Beyond Gridlock?

Beyond Gridlock?

Prospects for Governance in the Clinton Years — and After

Report on a conference held in Washington, D.C., February 24, 1993, sponsored by the Committee on the Constitutional System and the Brookings Institution

James L. Sundquist, *Editor*

The Brookings Institution
Washington, D.C.

₿ THE BROOKINGS INSTITUTION

The Brookings Institution is an independent organization devoted to nonpartisan research, education, and publication in economics, government, foreign policy, and the social sciences generally. Its principal purposes are to aid in the development of sound public policies and to promote public understanding of issues of national importance.

The Institution was founded on December 8, 1927, to merge the activities of the Institute for Government Research, founded in 1916, the Institute of Economics, founded in 1922, and the Robert Brookings Graduate School of Economics and Government, founded in 1924.

The Board of Trustees is responsible for the general administration of the Institution, while the immediate direction of the policies, program, and staff is vested in the President, assisted by an advisory committee of the officers and staff. The by-laws of the Institution state: "It is the function of the Trustees to make possible the conduct of scientific research, and publication, under the most favorable conditions, and to safeguard the independence of the research staff in the pursuit of their studies and in the publication of the results of such studies. It is not a part of their function to determine, control, or influence the conduct of particular investigations or the conclusions reached."

The President bears final responsibility for the decision to publish a manuscript as a Brookings book. In reaching his judgment on the competence, accuracy, and objectivity of each study, the President is advised by the director of the appropriate research program and weighs the views of a panel of expert outside readers who report to him in confidence on the quality of the work. Publication of a work signifies that it is deemed a competent treatment worthy of public consideration but does not imply endorsement of conclusions or recommendations.

The Institution maintains its position of neutrality on issues of public policy in order to safeguard the intellectual freedom of the staff. Hence interpretations or conclusions in Brookings publications should be understood to be solely those of the authors and should not be attributed to the Institution, to its trustees, officers, or other staff members, or to the organizations that support its research.

Foreword

The 1992 election expressed a deep dissatisfaction in the American electorate with the way in which their national government had been working—or failing to work. The discontent was commonly directed at what was called "gridlock," a term relatively new to the country's political vocabulary.

During the campaign, journalists and pollsters alike reported that the voters were in an angry mood, hostile toward incumbents in general and politicians as a class. The hostility had been intensified by a series of scandals in both houses of Congress. But the anger arose from deeper causes: from a sense that the president and the Congress were failing to cope with urgent national needs at the same time they were running budgetary deficits of intolerable size and burdening the country with a national debt that had reached a level both economically dangerous and morally unacceptable.

In the election, not only did the voters express their anti-incumbent, antipolitician mood by turning out of office the sitting president—for only the fourth time in a century that an elected president seeking reelection had been rejected. They also gave an astonishing 19 percent of the presidential vote to H. Ross Perot, a candidate who had never held public office and who conducted an eccentric, on-again-off-again campaign, but who represented the most drastic degree of change that was offered the electorate in 1992. An abnormally high proportion of House members chose to retire rather than face the hostile electorate, and others were defeated, with the result that the current House has the largest number of newcomers since 1948, about one-fourth of the total membership. Finally, fourteen states voted to arbitrarily limit the number of terms their representatives and senators could serve in Congress.

But the voters did one other thing: they ended a period of divided government that had lasted for twelve years and for twenty of the preceding twenty-four. During those years, a Republican president had confronted a Congress of which at least one house, and most of the time both houses, was controlled by the opposition Democrats. And the exit polls, taken as voters left their voting places on election day 1992, indicated that the citizenry had come to identify divided government as one cause of gridlock and hoped that governmental effectiveness would be restored with one-party control of both the presidency and the Congress.

The questions early in 1993 were, then, whether unified government under a single responsible—and accountable— party could indeed prove to be the solution to governmental gridlock and the accompanying loss of confidence of the public in its institutions. If so, how must the new president and the Congress conduct themselves to bring about that happy outcome? And whether or not it were so, what further reforms in the system might still be needed to improve the performance of the government?

To ponder these questions, the Committee on the Constitutional System and the Brookings Institution convened an all-day conference on February 24, 1993, exactly five weeks after the inauguration of President Bill Clinton. The participants included politicians of long experience, Washington journalists, political scientists, and other observers of the national political scene. This is a summary report of that conference, prepared by one of the participants, James L. Sundquist, who is both one of the original organizers of the committee a dozen years ago and a senior fellow emeritus at Brookings.

We express our gratitude particularly to Peter P. Schauffler, coordinator of the Committee on the Constitutional System since its formation, for his tireless work in planning and arranging the conference; to Thomas E. Mann, director of governmental studies at Brookings, and Jack DuVall for their advice on the conference format and the selection of participants; and to Hedrick Smith, distinguished political commentator, analyst, and author, for his artful service as moderator of the conference.

We also thank those who provided financial support for the conference and related activities—the Dillon Fund, the Ford Foundation, the Rockefeller Foundation, the CBS Foundation, the William and Flora Hewlett Foundation, the American Express Foundation, the Heinz Family Foundation, J. Irwin Miller, W. Thad Rowland, the John D. and Catherine T. MacArthur Foundation, and the Upjohn Company. And we acknowledge the indispensable skills of Robert Redd of the Federal News Service in transcribing the conference proceedings; of Inge Lockwood in typing and proofreading the entire manuscript; of Nancy Davidson in editing it; and of Susan Woollen and Norman Turpin in typesetting it.

In early 1995, after the adjournment of the first Clinton Congress and the midterm election, we expect to convene a second conference, with many of the same participants, to test the appraisals of the political system and the predictions offered in February 1993. We hope then to answer more definitively the question of whether the government has indeed moved beyond gridlock, has been fulfilling its responsibilities in a more effective manner, and by so doing has restored the public confidence and trust that are indispensable to a successfully functioning democracy.

Bruce K. MacLaury
President
The Brookings Institution

Lloyd N. Cutler
Co-Chairman
Committee on the
Constitutional System

Participants

Howard H. Baker, Jr.
U.S. senator, Republican of Tennessee, 1967–85, and Senate majority leader, 1981–85. White House chief of staff to President Reagan, 1987–88.

James MacGregor Burns
Professor emeritus of political science, Williams College. Author, nearly a score of books, including a Pulitzer Prize–winning biography of Franklin Roosevelt.

Lloyd N. Cutler
Co-chairman of the Committee on the Constitutional System. White House counsel to President Carter, 1979–81.

Thomas J. Downey
U.S. representative, Democrat of New York, 1975–93. Member, Ways and Means Committee, and congressional adviser to SALT II and START negotiations.

Kenneth M. Duberstein
Assistant to the president for legislative affairs, deputy chief of staff, and chief of staff to President Reagan, 1981–83, 1987–89. Director of congressional relations, General Services Administration, during Nixon administration and deputy under secretary of labor during Ford administration.

David Gergen
White House staff member, 1971–76; chief of research and writing for President Nixon and director of communications for President Ford. White House director of communications for President Reagan, 1981–83. (Joined President Clinton's White House staff, June 1993.)

Celinda Lake

Pollster, tactician, and adviser for Democratic party committees and candidates. Author, *Public Opinion Polling: A Manual for Public Interest Groups* (1986).

Jim Leach

U.S. representative, Republican of Iowa. Member, U.S. delegation to Geneva disarmament conference, 1971–72.

Thomas E. Mann

Director, Governmental Studies program, Brookings Institution. Co-director, AEI-Brookings Renewing Congress Project.

Andrea Mitchell

Radio and television journalist. White House correspondent, 1981–88, and chief White House correspondent since 1989, NBC News.

Thomas Oliphant

Washington correspondent, *Boston Globe*. Author, *All by Myself*, an account of the 1988 presidential campaign (1989).

Howard Paster

Congressional liaison director, White House, for President Clinton. Staff member on Capitol Hill, both House and Senate, 1967–77.

Joseph L. (Jody) Powell

Press secretary, White House, for President Carter, 1977–81. Washington columnist, *Los Angeles Times*, and news analyst, ABC News, 1982–87.

Corinne (Cokie) Roberts

Washington correspondent, ABC News, National Public Radio. Member of executive committee, Radio and TV Correspondents Association, for eight years since 1980, including presidency in 1981.

Donald L. Robinson

Professor of government, Smith College. Research director, Committee on the Constitutional System, and author, *Government for the Third American Century* (1989).

Warren B. Rudman
U.S. senator, Republican of New Hampshire, 1981–92. Co-chair, the Concord Coalition, a public interest group founded in 1993 to advocate fiscal and budget reform.

Barbara Sinclair
Professor of political science, University of California at Riverside. Author, *Transformation of the U.S. Senate* (1989), winner of Fenno and Hardeman prizes.

Hedrick Smith
New York Times reporter and editor, 1962–88; Moscow bureau chief, 1971–74, Washington bureau chief, 1976–79; chief Washington correspondent, 1979–85. Author, *The Power Game: How Washington Works* (1988).

Steven S. Smith
Professor of political science, University of Minnesota, and former senior fellow, Brookings Institution. Author, *Call to Order: Floor Politics in the House and Senate* (1989).

James L. Sundquist
Senior fellow emeritus, Brookings Institution. Author, *Constitutional Reform and Effective Government* (rev. ed. 1992).

Contents

Beyond Gridlock?

1 The Questions

"We meet at an auspicious and fascinating moment of American history," said moderator Hedrick Smith in opening the February 24, 1993, conference organized by the Committee on the Constitutional System and the Brookings Institution to look back on the era of divided government that had been ended—at least temporarily—by the 1992 election of President Bill Clinton and to assess the prospects of the government newly unified under the control of the Democratic party and installed in office a few weeks earlier. Smith continued:

For only the second time in twenty-four years, all three political arms of the government—the House, the Senate, and the White House—have been placed in the hands of the same political party. That suggests that we are at—choose your metaphor—a watershed, a turning point, a moment when the pendulum of history is ready to swing back in the opposite direction. Or are we? There is a constant debate among aficionados of American politics as to whether the flaws and problems that we see day in and day out, week in and week out, are those of personality and of miscues, or whether they point to more fundamental difficulties in our system that, as some here believe, require major structural reforms.

Today, we will be looking at whether there are far deeper problems in our temple of democracy that would suggest that Bill Clinton, for all his energy and all the enthusiasm he stirred among the public as a candidate, may be headed for a fall, not because of any problems of his own, but because the system simply will not respond even to aggressive, assertive, and knowledgeable leadership by a president who has his party allies in control of both houses of Congress.

1

In his keynote address, Lloyd Cutler, co-chairman of the Committee on the Constitutional System, linked the public's dissatisfaction with government—as evidenced in the 1992 election—to the country's experience during the preceding two decades of divided government when the White House and the Congress were controlled by opposing political parties most of the time. Said Cutler:

For the past twenty years or so, most Americans have been deeply disappointed in the quality of the national government. They have deplored the mounting deficits, the flattening out of economic growth, the rise in crime, drug abuse, and homelessness. And above all, they have deplored the deadlock between the president and the Congress, the divisive influence of huge campaign contributions from well-heeled interest groups, and the tendency of most elected politicians to claim, as individuals, that although the results they collectively produce are admittedly very poor, "Not I, but some other set of politicians is responsible for the outcomes."

Some observers inside and outside the Beltway have noted that this high level of public dissatisfaction coincides with a historically high frequency of divided government. The president and a majority in one or both houses of Congress have been of opposing parties for twenty of the last twenty-four years. In contrast, in only three out of twenty-five presidential elections in the nineteenth century did the winning presidential candidate fail to carry a majority of both houses for his party. And there was no such occasion in the twentieth century until Dwight Eisenhower's reelection in 1956. But in the nine presidential elections from 1956 through 1988, we chose divided government six times.

This remarkable coincidence between public dissatisfaction and divided government may well have played a part in the 1992 election. During the 1980s, as political scientists and pollsters all know, public opinion polls had indicated that the public thought it good to have a president of one party and a majority in Congress of the other party. During the 1992 campaign, however, public opinion may well have shifted.

All three candidates were publicly critical of divided government and the gridlock it produced. Governor Clinton, very naturally, pointed out that, since the long-standing congressional majorities in Congress were unlikely to be overturned, the problem could best be solved by electing a Democratic president. President Bush replied that a better solution would be to reelect him and return Republican majorities in Congress. And Ross Perot, of course, argued for a no-party government. When the voters chose the Clinton solution of a unified Democratic government, the exit polls, taken on election day, suggested that one important reason was public concern about four more years of divided government and the gridlock it produces.

But does the return of a united government mean that the deadlocks between the president and Congress are over, that the government will now decisively improve its performance, and that public satisfaction with governmental institutions will thereupon improve? Most of us will probably start out and finish with the hypothesis that "it ain't necessarily so." But we will probably disagree as to why and as to the structural and tactical measures the president and his party colleagues in the congressional leadership need to take to make even a united government work.

For example, should the president formulate his legislative program in collaboration with the legislative leadership, and make whatever modifications are necessary to win its support? Or should he stick with his own ideas and go over the heads of his own party's congressional leaders to bring public pressure on them to enact his program?

And if the president and the Democratic party leadership agree on the program, should the leadership get tougher with the party rank and file? And even if the leadership wanted to, can it nowadays offer the incentives or threaten the penalties necessary to line up the votes? Should Democratic majorities in Congress return to the Woodrow Wilson style of caucus—sometimes characterized as "King Caucus"—in which a majority of the Democrats in a house could bind their colleagues to vote with them on any major issue? Is anything like that even remotely feasible today, when members have their own direct sources of campaign financing and are far less interested in the guidance of the party leaders than in the mail, telephone, and fax messages they receive spontaneously or otherwise from their constituents?

Would drastic changes in our campaign financing laws make a difference? And if so, can they possibly be enacted?

Would we have less gridlock if we adopted limits on the number of terms senators and congressmen can serve—the new cure being prescribed for what ails the government?

Have we entered the era of the electronic town meeting, in which the president can persuade his party colleagues in Congress only if he persuades the public and motivates them to call or write their members? What skills and allies does the president need to turn this electronic bully pulpit to his own advantage?

Underlying all these specific questions is the fundamental, and most important, issue of our time: In the social and technological context of the 1990s, even with a president and congressional majorities of the same party, can we make our national government work?

Democratic pollster Celinda Lake analyzed the mood of the electorate in 1992 and the meaning of that year's election:

This election was very much about change. Voters expressed in a number of ways their enormous appetite for change. It helped them choose a president. It helped them elect a record number of women candidates. It helped them make what they thought were some of the most dramatic statements they could by, for example, electing to the Senate Carol Moseley-Braun, an African American woman from Chicago, as a way of saying as vividly as possible, "This election is not going to be about politics as usual; this is not going to be more of the same." The voters wanted bold change, not tinkering at the margins.

The election was dominated by two contradictory emotions. On the one hand, there was enormous cynicism, reflected first and foremost among Perot voters, but really more broadly than that. On the other hand, hope was the single biggest emotion that voters expressed when they voted for Bill Clinton. They hoped for change on a number of fronts: the economy, moving this country forward, government tackling problems, setting this country in the right direction when something was fundamentally wrong, and reforming government, which had seemed incapable of changing.

People also voted for political reform. They wanted to change in a very fundamental way the way government works. They wanted government to pay attention to ordinary people. Voters came into 1992 thinking the worst of politicians ever, even worse than during the Watergate era. A third of voters today believe their own member of Congress could be a crook; 89 percent believe that government benefits special interests, not ordinary people; and 60 percent of people today believe that government is operated for the benefit of the few, not the majority.

The Democratic argument for activist government was most persuasive when it started out with a critique of government. One of the reasons that 60 percent of voters today think that Bill Clinton is a new kind of Democrat who is changing the direction of the Democratic party is that he has been forthright in saying that government has failed. You will hear the phrase again and again that government has failed the middle class, it has failed the people who play by the rules.

The voters also sought a renewal of energy from young leaders. This need was felt intensely by young voters, and if older voters were hesitant because they thought, "This is putting our kids in charge!" they still felt it was time to give those young people with energy a chance.

In voters' minds, the economy was the most vivid example of the failure of government. This was a different kind of recession to voters. It was a much more profound recession to voters than to experts. Voters have consistently felt—particularly women voters—that conditions were much worse than the experts measured, as bad as those measurements were.

A couple of statistics will suggest why people felt so bad. First, two-thirds of Americans today believe that their children will not be better off than they are. Second, 60 percent of

Americans who are not of retirement age believe their retirement will be worse than their parents'. These are both profound violations of the American dream and, therefore, profound indictments of the political system.

Blue-collar America feels in desperate shape. Blue-collar America perceives itself as a group of people who started sweeping the floors of General Motors and moved up to shop steward, and they believe that path is no longer available to their children, or maybe even to themselves. In focus groups, people say, "Ten years ago, if you lost your job in Willow Run you moved to Texas. If you lose your job in Willow Run today you've got to move to Kyoto." And blue-collar Americans know that they and their children cannot do that.

As for white-collar America, it has felt secure in its own and its families' future. Now, in this recession white-collar workers found themselves laid off and, most devastating of all, their sons and daughters coming back home with college degrees but without jobs and going back to their bedrooms.

Yet voters saw no action to deal with the economy as they personally experienced it. They rejected twelve years of Reaganomics; in fact, as the election season began, Ronald Reagan was more unpopular than Jimmy Carter. But the people saw no alternative theory to Reaganomics being offered.

They were concerned about health care, and while voters did not have a great deal of faith in government, they thought the private sector had so failed in health care that even government would be a better solution than the insurance companies.

They were concerned about the deficit—Perot voters in particular—not only because it represented money but because it represented more than anything else politics-as-usual in Washington, a system that basically did not work or operate by commonsense rules that any fool could figure out.

On election day, Clinton's strongest advantages were being for change and for getting things done. Those were the keys to his success, and they are the key to the relative benevolence of voters now as they look toward his plan.

Let me explain further the voters' profound sense of failed representation. At the core of it is special interests. People think the system has failed when money talks louder than ordinary people. Even ordinary people who are yelling at their elected officials and calling and faxing them in record numbers still think that money talks louder than they do, that special interests have turned politics into the defense of particularized interests rather than the common interest, and have contributed to gridlock and to partisan bickering.

They saw the power of special interests most vividly illustrated in the savings and loan bailout. Even though voters do not talk about it very much, that bailout is still a flash point. Then came the congressional pay raise, which voters are still furious about. The pay raise said to the voter, "The really dirty story here is that elected officials are representing themselves, not me, and they are doing it at my expense." It said that members of Congress had somehow created a special class for themselves, an elite class. They had become a special interest of their own.

While voters have a profound sense of cynicism and a desire for change, their concerns are still quite diffuse. When we asked voters about a month ago, "What is the biggest problem in Washington?" 15 percent said special interests; 19 percent said corruption and ethics; 20 percent said partisan bickering; 17 percent said not representing people. But even if people do not know the overall change that they want, they are very clear about some things they would like to see.

First, they would like to see special interests out of politics. They respond to anything that seems to them to be cutting back the influence of special interests, whether that is registering lobbyists, taxing them, banning political action committees, or whatever.

Second, they want an end to perks and privileges. They are profoundly tired of elected officials who elevate themselves above ordinary people. While we talk about class warfare as being between the rich and the middle class, in the public's mind—as anxious as they are to tax the wealthy—the real class warfare is between elected officials and regular people.

Third, they want new people in office. There is a contradiction here, because they normally reelect incumbents, but even so they responded in 1992 to the idea of diversity. They liked the notion that government would look more like the American public. One reason they want to limit campaign spending is to bring in new faces. That they thought of Bill Clinton as an outsider explained part of his popularity. The desire for new people in office is also one of the motivations behind term limits. Voters are not particularly intense about term limits, even though they will almost always vote for them as a reform that they think will bring change.

Fourth, they want to cut waste. The voters used to see waste only in programs they did not like, such as welfare and foreign aid. Today, voters think that forty-four cents of every dollar is wasted, even a third of social security. That does not mean they want to cut social security by one-third, but people now believe even their most favorite programs have significant waste.

Where does that leave us? The American public is devoted to change and it believes the problems in the way politics operate are not superficial but fundamental. They do not have a very clear sense of how to bring about that change, other than to hammer the system. The Perot voters are most intent on that, flailing at the system in hopes that it will respond but cynical about the prospects. In contrast, Clinton voters are optimistic that the system will respond. But all voters need to get a sense of what they should do to really make this system work.

White House staffer David Gergen suggested that, because the weakness of government is evident not just in the United States but in other major democracies as well, and because the loss of public confidence extends beyond government to other societal institutions, "deeper forces" may be at work:

As we look abroad and see what is happening with other democratic governments and other industrialized nations, one is struck by the weakness of them all. One cannot name, looking beyond this country, a single strong government among the major industrial democracies, and their troubles have persisted since the early 1970s. All this suggests that even as we look at reforms, which are so necessary, even as we look at ways to overhaul our campaign finance laws, which we must do, even as we look at ways of strengthening our parties, which we must do, deeper forces may be at work that we should be aware of.

The basic forces are the economic gale winds that have been passing through the industrial world. Wages have gone down in many countries as they have faced global competition, productivity levels have fallen, and savings rates have gone down everywhere. The problems in the economy, I suggest, have caused greater public pessimism and cynicism about all the institutions in our life, not just government. All major institutions in the industrialized nations—not just our presidents—have lost credibility and authority. Our university presidents, our religious leaders, our business leaders do not speak with the same authority they did twenty-five years ago, and that is true in other nations as well.

The publics are also far better educated. Far more people have had university educations and wish to participate in the discussion. Most of us think that is healthier, but we must understand that it is also messier. The people are not passive anymore. They want to have a voice about what is affecting them. That slows the process down and makes accomplishing things more difficult, but it is something we should accept and come to appreciate.

Representative Jim Leach, Republican of Iowa, dissented from the emphasis being given to gridlock as a problem and as an important factor in the 1992 election:

This discussion absolutely misperceives the import of the gridlock issue. And that misperception is the basis for some misguided solutions to an exaggerated problem.

This last election was about boredom and generational politics, not gridlock. President Bush lost because he was perceived to be bored with the problems of the American people, and because he was out of touch with youth in particular.

The reason for the split government of the immediate past has been threefold. One, there is an instinct in the American body politic to favor checks and balances. Two, in close elections many Americans give the benefit of the doubt to legislative candidates with a soft heart and executives with hard-headed capacities to govern. And in close contests this generally means Democrats in legislative offices, Republicans in the executive. Three, the new breed of Democratic political professional is far more adept at the art of legislative politics than are Republican candidates.

Of these three reasons, the second is the most important—that is, the public likes soft-hearted legislators—but this may be in transition. My sense is that the Perot movement may have longer-term implications for legislative races than for the presidential, and it is conceivable the '90s may find the public reversing itself and opting for more conservative legislators to balance more liberal executives.

But as backdrop in discussing the gridlock problem, we should keep in mind that our political parties are far closer to each other in outlook than those of any other western or eastern democracy, and, with the exception of the deficit, have not been totally unsuccessful in working out their differences. The problem in Washington is not that elected officials have ignored public concerns and failed to respond, but that they have been too responsive. The country wants more programs and lower taxes, and leaders of both parties and both branches of government have worked together to provide bread and circuses. The problem is not gridlock; it is lack of backbone, the pandering incapacities of elected officials to say "no."

2 The Prospect for Ending Gridlock

In their predictions as to whether the restoration of unified party government would indeed bring an end to gridlock, the conference participants ranged across the spectrum from optimism to gloom. Thomas Mann, director of governmental studies at Brookings, presented perhaps the most hopeful assessment of the prospect for a fruitful collaboration between the executive and legislative branches during the Clinton years, while Kenneth Duberstein, formerly of the Reagan White House staff, made the case for expecting an early renewal of feuding between the president and the Congress despite the ties of their common Democratic partisanship. Other participants took positions in between, and some, of course, took the view that, with Democrats in control of both branches, gridlock might even be something to be desired. Mann said:

There is an insider's view of the Clinton presidency—and all those insiders do not reside within the Beltway—that this presidency is doomed to fail. That assessment is based on a number of considerations, among them:

—a fragile electoral base;

—the absence of a mandate with which to govern;

—a string of broken campaign promises, with the middle-class tax cut being the most prominent;

—a set of concerns about the disingenuousness of the new president and his administration—as reporters in Washington say, too clever by half;

—a belief that deep divisions among congressional Democrats will come to the fore on the important policy problems that the Clinton administration tries to grapple with, as will the almost certain united opposition from Republicans in both the House and Senate;

11

—a belief that the problems that confront the nation are so intractable, and there is so little public consensus on them, that it is impossible for this new president, in spite of the return of unified party government, to grapple successfullywith them;

—and a view that the president's program itself is inadequate to the task, even if somehow it came to be adopted.

Underlying all of these considerations is a perhaps even more telling proposition, which relates to the separation between campaigning and governing. This separation robs elections of two of their critical elements. One concerns the content of the campaign. Does it clarify choices for the country, build public support for new policy decisions, facilitate some kind of honest discussion between leaders and citizens? The other has to do with the means of governing. Does an election create a political basis for action in government through a sense of shared fate between the president and Congress?

In the best of all worlds, a successful presidential candidate would win a decisive victory, carry into office new or enhanced majorities in both houses of Congress who are committed to enacting a program that is attentive to the country's problems and that was clearly articulated during the course of the campaign. That is our model of how American democracy should work. I am all for it. It think it would be terrific if we had it.

But while this responsible party model is attractive, it seldom materializes in the real world of politics. In recent history, the elections of 1964 and 1980 came closest to it. But in 1992, the argument goes—and this is the sophisticated pessimist argument about the Clinton presidency—the election fell well short of that ideal. The election results were indecisive and fragile, the pessimists argue, a mere 43 percent plurality for the president. The president's party lost ten seats in the House and made no gain in the Senate. As for the content of the campaign, they contend, it was poor, because the specific plans that were offered neither added up nor addressed in any serious way the problems confronting the country.

From this prevalent view among the insiders I wish to register dissent. I believe it is too harsh and pessimistic a view of the election and of the prospects for the new administration. First, the 1992 election was much less threadbare than the 1960 or 1976 elections, the elections with which 1992 is typically compared. Yes, it fell short of 1964 and 1980, but in terms of both the content of the campaign and the decisiveness of the results, 1992 is somewhere in between the responsible party model elections of those years and the threadbare elections of 1960 and 1976, so that a potential exists for building something out of the 1992 election. Much of what was said in the campaign provides a reasonable base for governing. I do not see a great disjuncture between campaigning and governing.

Second, the return of unified party government is especially significant in 1992 as contrasted with 1960 and 1976. This time it follows an extended period of divided government—and conflictual divided government, which was really quite different from the earlier experiences—twelve years of it and, except for the four-year hiatus of the Carter presidency, an additional eight years since 1968.

Third, the parties today are stronger in the Congress. Democrats and Republicans are more unified. I would argue that Clinton's reduced majority in the House, compared to Carter's, is actually more potent a force because of the greater homogeneity among Democrats.

Fourth, there is a larger freshman class. That is a wild card in our politics that provides some possibilities that would not exist otherwise.

Fifth, the public anger is palpable. Members see it and they feel it.

Finally, there is a Democratic desperation to succeed, which was not apparent in early 1977 or early 1961. The whole political context has been transformed.

Mandates are not objective realities. They are fictions, stories told by successful candidates and sold successfully to other politicians and to the public. It is easier to sell a mandate the more decisive the election results and the more explicit the commitments made during the course of the campaign. The stuff with which President Clinton has to work is not as substantial as he would like, but stuff there is to fashion a mandate. The challenge is for him to construct one that is faithful to the central tenets of his campaign, that is attentive to the real problems facing the country, that is persuasive to members of the political community as well as to the public, and that is translatable into concrete proposals for government action.

I submit that a mandate responsive to the factors I have just identified is being fashioned, and that the adjustments that have been made from campaigning to governing have been largely constructive from a public policy point of view. And they have been openly acknowledged, which is an essential aspect of a president's transition from campaigning to governing. If he does not level, is not honest about what he is doing, he gets into trouble.

Clinton's program thus far, however susceptible to criticism as insufficiently ambitious and not composed of the right elements, seems attentive both to the substantive problems the country faces and to the need to build and maintain public support—an element shortchanged in discussions of governing.

I would not for a moment suggest that this presidency is certain to succeed. That would be foolhardy. There are enormous obstacles to successful governance—difficult public policy problems that require the imposition of short-term costs for long-term gains. Our society is deeply divided over these. And the separation of our political institutions makes the task truly daunting. But there is at least a possibility that this election may have set in motion a new dynamic that will make a difference in our politics.

First, we have a president playing offense, not defense, with the public, which means a willingness to try to shape public opinion and not simply respond to it, an effort to try to harness the plebiscitary pressures that are so transparent in our politics and channel them in ways that can lead to constructive public policy. I think we have a president who relishes engaging in that task.

Second, the president is willing to play offense with the Congress. Nothing leads to more deceit by members of Congress than a president's unwillingness to engage and to lead. And there is a broad ideological compatibility between the president and the majorities in Congress that has not been seen in a long while.

Third, the president and the Congress have more than the usual sense of shared political stakes. The congressional Democrats know that if this Clinton presidency fails they will be in deep trouble, that 1994 and 1996 will be very, very difficult years. It will not be enough for individual members of the House or the Senate to say "I did my level best" and then dissociate themselves from the collective product.

Fourth, the public is demanding policy resolution and results.

So, an element of party responsibility and accountability has returned to Washington. The Democrats may incur the almost united opposition of the Republican party, but that is the way some people believe government ought to work. Democrats ought to say what they believe and stand or fall on it. Adjustments and changes will be made in the president's program, but rather than weakening it or destroying it, the changes may well be positive from a public policy point of view.

More generally, I believe we may have reached the point of more honest discussion of problems and solutions. We saw signs of that in the State of the Union speech. The president's willingness to level with the people consistently, to be explicit, to be absolutely forthcoming when he has changed his position, will be crucial. His honesty will set the tone, will create the moral authority of his presidency. I think he is moving in a promising direction.

Howard Paster, as President Clinton's assistant in charge of congressional relations, summarized his grounds for optimism:

That we can now, with a Democratic majority on the Hill and a Democrat in the White House, govern successfully, I think will be borne out.

Bill Clinton is both the chief lobbyist in the White House and the best. He comes to Washington with a lot of experience as head of the National Governors' Association. In this city, he knows members of Congress well. While obviously the majorities will come from the Democratic side, the president will undertake to work with the Republicans as well, and I think that support will be there.

One of the hurdles we are dealing with is the fact that fewer than 30 percent of the Democratic members of the House have ever served before with a Democratic president, and they are learning how it works. We are learning too. It is a different kind of experience. We are very sensitive to the fact that there are a lot of Democrats with names like Rostenkowski, and Brooks, and Dingell, and Biden, and Byrd, who during a Republican administration may have enjoyed more comfort in terms of heading off on their own issues than they might feel with a Democratic president. There are also some very important leaders—people named Foley, and Mitchell, and Gephardt, and committee chairmen—for whom the new situation requires a change. We are working with all of them very closely.

When some of these people at a meeting were questioning somebody in the new administration, I said, "No, no, wait. It is no longer us and them, it is us and us." And they said, "You are right." Then they paused and said, "We have to remember that." And we need to remind them of that and remind ourselves. But the leadership has found it the easiest adjustment to make, the chairmen have done a good job of it, and the freshmen have been very supportive.

The biggest accommodation in getting Democrats to do business together will not be with the freshmen, because Clinton and Gore are part of the Class of 1992 and identify closely with it, nor with the most senior members, some of whom worked with Democratic presidents in the 1960s. Rather, it will be with folks who have been here for from four to maybe seven or eight terms, who might have been here for the last two years of the Carter administration but really have not been in this situation before. A lot of them are from marginal districts, and we have to be sensitive to their interests.

The time the president invested with them in his first five weeks in office is a measure of respect and a signal of his intentions to work with them. He invited every Democratic member of the House to the White House and then began inviting House Republicans. He visited the Senate Democratic party lunch. There were many, many smaller meetings. The president worked the phone an enormous amount of time, well into the evening. One of the key reasons that this Democratic president and Democratic Congress will succeed together is the realization—and they articulate it constantly—that they will be judged together. If the election was about ending gridlock—and I think it was in part—if it was about achieving change—and Bill Clinton uses that phrase all the time—then if we do not break the gridlock, if we do not achieve the change, the burden at the polls will be borne by all Democrats. This is something we understand very clearly. And based upon what we hear from the folks on the Hill, it is something they understand as well.

And so I continue to be optimistic—I could not do this job if I were not—that we will have a successful four years in which a Democratic president and a Democratic Congress work well together.

But Kenneth Duberstein was not persuaded. Reflecting on his years in the Reagan White House, he foresaw a recurrence of some degree of gridlock as inevitable in a government of separated institutions. Said Duberstein:

The good news is that on November 3 the American people clearly demonstrated that they want an end to gridlock, they want change, they want more accountability in our government—no excuses. The bad news is that now is about the best it gets.

I remember well that when Ronald Reagan was elected some of the pundits and some of the people on Capitol Hill said, "We finally have a president who understands and can work with the Congress, not like his predecessor, Jimmy Carter." They said that this was an end to gridlock and finally we were going to address the country's problems.

I remember eight years later—1989—and these same pundits were suggesting that in George Bush we finally had a president who understood the Congress because he used to serve on the Ways and Means Committee, he knew all the members by their first name, and he continued to play in the House gym.

And now, we have Bill Clinton, who in his initial weeks has done such an extraordinary job that the deadlock under George Bush has been turned into so-called expectations for action.

I also recall a conversation I had early in Ronald Reagan's

term with one of the top lobbyists for Jimmy Carter. I suggested that rounding up votes had turned out to be not all that tough. You put Ronald Reagan out in front because not only is he a great communicator, he is a great lobbyist. You put him out there with the American people and the Congress, you wrap yourself in the American flag, and the votes are there. And he said, "But wait till you are at 30 percent in the polls."

I hope the American people will not be disappointed, but I am concerned that the end of gridlock is unlikely. The system is biased toward gridlock, not toward action. It is far, far easier to block something on Capitol Hill than it is to pass something affirmatively.

Yes, I think Bill Clinton has used, and will continue to use, the tools at his disposal to try to end the gridlock and make unified government work. He clearly understands how crucial it is to use the bully pulpit of the Oval Office. A president must communicate directly with the American people and must articulate his visions and his ideas. He must sell them to the American public, and he must lobby for them. He must make his message clear, clean, short, crisp, repeated, and repeated, and repeated. He must keep his agenda focused and not laden with too many priorities. He must campaign for his program, as President Clinton has so far done extraordinarily well. This president certainly understands the need to give the Congress, especially the Democratic members, cover. And he certainly understands symbols.

But it is also important for everybody to face some realities. To be successful, a president must be both revered and feared, and Clinton is neither yet. Can he be challenged? Will he be willing to say no to some important Democratic constituency or some important members of the Democratic party on the Hill?

And Congress seems able to do only two things well: nothing, and overreact. The Hill has little leadership and even less followship, and there are very few incentives, let alone penalties, for the leadership to use. There are in reality 535 separate fiefdoms. The game is a fifteen-second soundbite. The game is not being part of the leadership's machine.

Clinton understands that the game for him is 218 votes in

the House and 50 in the Senate, and that he will need differing coalitions on each vote. But the Speaker and the majority leader can probably deliver their own vote and maybe a few others, but nowhere near 218. Unlike twenty or thirty years ago, in the House you need to get the votes one by one and not in big clusters.

Most representatives and senators do not feel beholden to any president, let alone one who ran behind them in the last election. I am reminded of advice I received from former Senator Jacob Javits of New York in his last year of life, when I was perplexed and trying to figure out a vote that had just taken place in the Senate. I asked him to explain why certain senators had voted a certain way. And with halting breath he said to me, "You must always realize that senators vote in a priority order. First, they vote for their states; second, they vote out of institutional loyalty to the Senate; and, third, if they have not decided on the basis of either of those, and the president happens to be of their own party, well maybe they will give him a vote. But the state or the district always comes first, the institution second, and only then the president."

Another thing to remember is how important back home is. They used to call Reagan the great lobbyist, but I remember sitting in the Oval Office as we lobbied not only in 1981, 1982, and 1983, but also in 1987 and 1988, and member after member would say, "Mr. President, I really want to support your package. The trouble is I am not hearing anything from back home." The key was to make sure that we explained why things were important to the district, and why the district really would support what Reagan wanted.

The bad news also is that once the president gets a vote he wants, the immediate instinct of most members is to cast the next vote to show their independence from the administration. This is especially true when you have asked them to vote for a big package, in which some provisions did not make sense for their districts but had to be swallowed as part of the overall package. Then their answer is, "I need the next vote to show that I am independent of the White House."

All these Democratic members have made their careers out

of opposing administrations, and now find they have to carry the water for, or at least support, an administration of their own party. It is not an easy transformation. They have to bury their own agendas.

When Howard Baker was Senate majority leader in 1981 he constantly referred to himself as the president's leader in the Senate, not simply the Senate's majority leader. As the president's person in the Senate, it was not easy to tell committee chairmen—some of whom for the first time finally had a committee—and other committee members that they had to wait on their agendas until they had taken up the president's.

One of the most important things that Clinton has to break gridlock, which we did not have, at least in the House, is the ability to control the timetable and the rules, to vote when you have the votes and not a minute before.

The American people really are rooting for Bill Clinton and rooting for our system of government to work. Yet in spite of both ends of Pennsylvania Avenue being controlled by the same political party, we still will have two competing governments— one on the Hill, one at the White House; one focused on the national interest, one focused on 435 separate districts or 50 states. The challenge for Bill Clinton is to find a way to preside over both. And I think the odds, at least institutionally, are against him.

Jody Powell, who served in a unified Democratic government as press secretary to President Carter, explains why President Clinton's prospects appear better than Carter's did:

In many ways the differences between the situation Jimmy Carter faced in 1977 and the situation now are more striking than the similarities. Let me start with the mood of the country. In 1977, even though the electorate had defeated an incumbent president and installed a president of a different party, there was no great sense of unrest, anger, or fear. But this time, people are upset, and they are angry, and a lot of them are scared.

Coming from that, there was no real sense in 1977 that the country was dying to get anything specific done. The electorate had sent no particular message, even though a lot of things needed to be done. The campaign itself did not provide any clear direction in terms of "By God, this is what we want done here," either to the Congress or to the administration.

What we decided to make our primary effort in that first year was, as you will recall, a national energy policy. But, as I said, there was no great sense in the country that we really needed a national energy policy. Maybe there should have been. We had been through a couple of oil shocks with considerable damage to the economy. But in fact the first task that faced the Carter administration was to convince people that we at least had a problem that needed to be dealt with.

When President Carter stood up and said that we faced what he called "the moral equivalent of war," a lot of folks, particularly in this town, snickered. A couple of years later, when oil prices quadrupled, particularly the folks who lost their jobs were not snickering anymore. And I suppose two years ago, when we went to war over oil, other people quit snickering. But at the time we could not convince everybody that it was a serious problem. Now, of course, everyone recognizes that it is.

Another difference, as I think back to those times, is that Congress as an institution was riding rather high in 1977. Congress had gotten a lot of good press. It was given a great deal of the credit, and perhaps justifiably so, for bringing us through Watergate and all of that. There was a sense that, while some things had gone wrong, on the whole the system had worked. Democrats in the Congress had seen that big influx of Watergate babies in 1975, and that looked pretty good to them. The Democrats in Congress and the traditional Democratic constituencies—not every single one but as a general rule—had no sense in 1977 that they really had much of a stake in the success of the Carter administration. A lot of Democrats then seemed to believe that God had pretty well made up His mind that this country was supposed to have a Democrat in the White House and Democrats controlling both houses of Congress for the rest of this century, at least. So they saw Jimmy Carter's election as a return to normalcy.

I think there is an understanding now among constituency

groups and among Democrats on the Hill that they do have a real stake in the success of this administration, particularly on the core issues of the economy and deficit reduction. Yet I say that with my fingers a bit crossed. I get the sense that they know it in their heads and maybe in their hearts, but their knees still jerk to the same old rhythm and they sometimes cannot help themselves when it comes down to the specifics of implementation.

But I believe that both Democrats and Republicans have a stake. My guess is that if substantial things do not happen, particularly on the deficit and the economy, that if gridlock continues, the fate of incumbents of both parties in 1994 will make what happened in 1992 seem something like a stroll in the park. While the Republicans would no doubt benefit as a party, that would not be much help to individual Republicans who are now incumbents, because they would be in the cross hairs too.

That sets up what I think is an opportunity for the Clinton administration. Will it work in practice? About all I can say is that these folks have some things working in their favor that are not insignificant. They have a better chance of making the system work. If they cannot, we will have some really angry people out there who are going to be willing in 1994, and maybe in 1996 too, to vote for whomever they can find who is as far away as possible from this town and the institutions and processes they have seen in the past. Under these circumstances, by 1996 we could be looking at Ross Perot as the moderate responsible guy who will be our only hope for stopping some certifiable lunatic who is running ten points ahead of the pack.

Reflecting on his years in the Reagan White House, David Gergen saw President Clinton as weaker than Reagan in some respects but strong in others:

One of the reasons that I and some others joined up with Ronald Reagan in 1980 and went into the White House was that we were terribly concerned about the strength of the presidency. Between 1960 and 1980, none of the five presidents had successfully completed two terms and some of them had left in dis-

grace or defeat. So we came into the Reagan administration feeling that this might be the last chance to restore the presidency
and govern successfully with it.

And for a time in the Reagan presidency, even with the
House of Representatives controlled by the other party, it still
seemed possible to have a strong presidency and to govern. Yet
now we are asking, "Were those brief years an aberration? Are
we returning to a period in which it is much more difficult to
govern?"

But one factor that puts Clinton in a weak position, compared to Reagan, is what happened on election day. Of the five
Democratic presidents in this century before Bill Clinton, three
had successful legislative records and two, I would argue, were
less successful. The three who had successful legislative records
were Woodrow Wilson and Franklin Roosevelt in their first
terms and Lyndon Johnson after 1964. The two who were less
successful were John Kennedy and Jimmy Carter. Now what
distinguished the three from the two? The three all came in with
big coattails and, therefore, had a lot of respect on Capitol Hill.
Most of them ran ahead of the people of their own party who
were elected to the Congress—ahead of the members in their
own districts—and that is what helped.

What distinguished Ronald Reagan was that when he was
elected in 1980 he brought enough Republican senators with
him to capture control of the Senate. Moreover, the fact that
many southern Democrats in the House ran behind Reagan in
their own districts gave him enormous strength. There was a
fear of Reagan—even an awe—and, believe me, those do make
a difference in politics. It did not last forever, of course. But Bill
Clinton did not bring Democrats in with him. He did not have
those coattails, and that is one reason he was having more trouble in dealing with the Congress as his term began.

Given that, he had to look to others in the game. He skillful-
ly looked to the public, and the public was more favorable than
it has been for most new presidents, including Jimmy Carter.
The public was much more ready for change, the kind of
change that Bill Clinton was pursuing. As David Broder of the
*Washington Post*t wrote, however, if there seemed to be an incon-

sistency between the message of the campaign and the message of the presidency, if there seemed to be a slipperiness in some of the things that were proposed, that could deeply cut into the public trust and the people's willingness to support the president.

As for the press, it has fallen in and out of love with Bill Clinton on several occasions. I think we brutalized Clinton in the early primaries a year ago. Later, during the general election period, on the whole we tilted toward Clinton. I do not think that cost George Bush the election, as some Republicans argue, but I do think there was a tilt. Then, in the transition and in the early weeks of the Clinton administration, some disenchantment appeared. But beginning with his State of the Union address, the press was wowed by how well Bill Clinton had captured the country. We will no doubt see the pendulum swing several more times.

However, the question is not whether the press reveres or fears the president but what the country at large senses and thinks about him. The country has no fear of him nor does it hold him reverentially, but he has been successful in speaking responsively to people's everyday concerns, and for the first time in recent years they have a president who cares. But, to repeat, they must also trust him if he is to establish that mystical bond with the people that Reagan enjoyed for a long time— beginning with the attempted assassination and lasting until it snapped in the Iran-contra affair. The critically important question is, if Bill Clinton has trouble in the Congress, what can he do with the people?

How you feel about the issue of divided government, about whether you want a president who can effectively ram things through Congress depends a lot, of course, on who is in charge and what your partisan persuasion is. Many on the Republican side are now saying, "Why do we want a government in which the president can ram things through? Why would we want an economic plan to go through in sixty days?"

I happen to think that we should not pass health care reform in ninety days, or one hundred days, or six months. It would be a serious mistake to try to reform an industry that amounts to 14 percent of the gross national product without public understanding of what is at stake, and that understanding does not exist now. If our system of checks and balances forces a longer debate, we may avoid what happened in catastrophic health care reform, when the public did not know what was going on, caught up with the bill later, and then forced the Congress into a humiliating reversal. So there are areas of our national life where we have not yet had full debate, where a little slowness, in my judgment, is healthy.

James Sundquist shared the optimistic outlook first expressed by Thomas Mann:

If the government cannot succeed in the present configuration, when can it possibly ever succeed? As Joan Quigley, the former official astrologer, might have said, the stars are really aligned right for the next four years.

The country has finally gotten back to unified government. For the first time in twelve years, somebody is going to be responsible. In the last three election campaigns, the Republican president has been able to say, "Don't blame me, blame those Democrats in control of Congress." And Democrats have been able to say, "Don't blame us, blame the president." Now the day of buck passing and blame shifting is over. The Democrats asked for complete responsibility for the government and got it. They know they are going to be held accountable, and on Capitol Hill they know they have to stick together and make a record.

The business of political parties is to oppose each other, to defeat each other, to discredit each other, all of which is normal and healthy. But when different parties control different elements of the government, this healthful competition is transmuted into conflict between the institutions of government themselves. For anything constructive to happen, three centers of power—the president, the Senate, and the House—have to get together. But when they are controlled by different parties, they do what comes naturally—that is, the institutions attempt to defeat, discredit, and undermine the work of one another. So we have been hearing the president castigating the Congress as dominated by spendthrifts and wastrels and the Congress, in turn, denouncing the president for lack of leadership. The recriminations flow back and forth between the ends of Pennsylvania Avenue and, as they insult one another, in the end the public comes to believe both sides. That has a lot to do, I believe, with the loss of confidence that the people have in their government.

For those of us who think that divided government has been at the heart of our governmental problems in the last twelve, or twenty-four years, the end of it is a momentous, profound change that could make a world of difference.

A further reason for optimism, which Tom Mann also mentioned, is that the Democratic party is much more homogeneous than it has been in anybody's memory. Skeptics about the significance of unified government like to point out that it did not work all that well under Jimmy Carter or John Kennedy or Harry Truman. But what they overlook is the fundamental shift that has taken place in the composition of the Democratic party. Thirty years ago, the South was represented by people like Harry Byrd, Howard Smith, James Eastland, Richard Russell, and Spessard Holland, whose philosophy was Republican and who voted with the Republicans. When at least one Democratic committee chairman, Senator Willis Robertson of Virginia, was unable to come to a meeting, he left his proxy not with his Democratic colleagues but with the Republicans. But people like that do not represent the South anymore. You cannot count anybody in the Senate who is of the stripe of Byrd, Eastland, or Russell. Now coming from the South as Democrats are moderates such as Wyche Fowler and Terry Sanford—who, I recognize, were defeated—but others, such as Bob Graham, who survived. The typical southern Democrat in both houses nowadays is ideologically comfortable with the mainstream of the Democratic party and with the president that party chose.

The third cause for optimism is what we have seen of the personal leadership capacity of the president. He has the political skills necessary for working with the Congress. He loves the political game. He is willing to put in the time and engage in small talk. He certainly has the energy and the knowledge. I worry a bit that the party programs are announced by the president unilaterally as his programs, without the input beforehand from the Congress that would command its loyalty thereafter out of a sense of coauthorship. But we will wait to see whether that becomes a habit—and a problem.

Representative Leach observed:

If Bill Clinton has an Achilles' heel, it will not be his savvy political ability and his capacity to end the gridlock. It will be the question of moral stature, whether he has the leadership ability to pull the country together not just with good ideas but also with a good example.

3 Political Party Reform

James MacGregor Burns has long argued that the American constitutional system is normally in a state of gridlock, broken only by occasional bursts of creative action. If even so masterful a politician as Franklin Roosevelt could not lead effectively after his first term, argued Burns (author of a prize-winning biography of FDR), the system must be faulty. But given the arduous process of amending the Constitution, and the unlikelihood that any fundamental change is possible, Burns offered as his reform agenda a series of proposals to strengthen political parties that could be accomplished simply by the parties themselves. This provoked a lively exchange of views with Representative Leach. Burns presented his case:

When some of us are rather pessimistic about a particular administration, it is not because we want to be but because we have seen the government in a situation of deadlock over and over again.

Even the master politician Franklin Roosevelt found governance so difficult during his second term that he first tried to reform the sacred Supreme Court, then went south during the mid-term election of 1938 to try to purge conservative, reactionary Democrats from the Congress, then took on the Democratic party to change it and the bureaucracy as well. That extremely skillful politician ended up frustrated by the system, and only the coming of World War II made it possible for Roosevelt to pull out of his political difficulties and, ironically, to provide in wartime a second New Deal that accomplished many of the things in areas such as housing, employment, and women's rights that he could not achieve before.

As I look back on the fifty years since, I would argue that

29

only during periods of crisis has it been possible for the government to unite. Certainly that is not a recipe for the future. If it takes crises of the magnitude of World War II or the civil rights struggle to pull us together, that is a dangerously weak basis for a governing system.

So, I propose some drastic remedies, controversial ones, affecting our political parties. There has been a running debate within the Committee on the Constitutional System as to whether the road to reform runs through party change or constitutional change. It has been not an unhappy debate but a constructive one. Some of us believe more in the party route, some more in the constitutional route, but it is a matter of emphasis because most of us would like to see a combination of the two. I myself have shifted back and forth over the years, sometimes hopeful about the constitutional route. But when I reflect on the difficulties of the amending process in this country and the opposition of the American people to any fundamental change in the Constitution, which they revere as sacred writ, I am so pessimistic about the possibilities of constitutional reform that I turn back to party reform as the more promising prospect.

The Founders were themselves divided on essentially this same question. It is quite remarkable that when many of the same men who wrote the Constitution that fragmented power so brilliantly took that power, they built in the 1790s a party system designed to reunite power to make it possible to govern. By 1800 a full-fledged two-party system was in being.

During most of the life of the nation since then, the constitutional fragmentation of governmental power has been balanced by the party strategy of knitting the executive, the legislature, and to some extent the judiciary together in order to achieve party aims. The system was therefore in a rather creative balance during most of our history. At times the party strategy clearly prevailed, particularly during the long period during the late nineteenth century when the Republican party generally was able to unite the government behind its goals.

In this century, however, that balance has been destroyed, as constitutional dispersion of power has continued and even intensified while the strength of parties has steadily ebbed. The reasons for the erosion of party power—the introduction of the party primary, the decline and fall of the party machines, the rise of antiparty attitudes, the impact of the electronic media, the channeling of political money to political action committees and candidates rather than to parties—have long been analyzed and need not be discussed here. But at the present rate of decline, in my pessimistic estimate, political parties as we know them—at least outside of Washington—will have virtually disappeared within the next quarter century as effective mechanisms. My question is, can they be restored as key mechanisms for uniting government and combating gridlock at the national, state, and local levels? I suggest only by the boldest and most creative kind of action, the same kind of bold and creative action the Framers undertook. I propose a series of steps to that end.

First of all, both parties should convene charter conventions to consider and mandate party reform. The Democrats once had a charter convention that met in Kansas City. It was a most amazing, remarkable convention, but as you might expect, it came to nothing as a way of restructuring the party. I propose that there be further charter conventions that would have the same power to restructure parties as constitutional conventions have to restructure government.

These are some crucial steps that charter conventions could take through party channels or through recommendations to legislatures:

—First, establish as the very foundation of the party at its grass roots, participatory democratically selected caucuses with power to choose all party officials including all convention delegates.

—Second, select all party nominees in democratically chosen nominating conventions, not just candidates for president and vice president but those for all other elective offices as well.

—Third, channel all political money obtained from federal or other public sources to political parties for internal organizational, educational, and leadership recruitment purposes. Money for campaign purposes should not be given directly to candidates but should be channeled through parties at every level.

—Fourth, elect national party chairpersons through open and democratic procedures at annual or biennial party conventions. The present practice whereby presidents pick national party chairs as freely and even as casually as they choose White House staff assistants should be scrapped as a grotesque perversion of party autonomy and party democracy. I have never been able to accept the idea that the great parties, with their historic role in this country, should turn belly up when they place a new man in the White House, one who may have had practically nothing to do with the party organization or the party structure, and supplicate him to designate someone to lead the party.

—Fifth, in between the party nominating conventions that choose candidates, hold, annually or every two years, conventions that discuss issues and write party platforms.

—And sixth, hold party charter conventions at least every twenty years to review and modernize party structure, organization, and processes.

The most important, radical, and controversial of these proposals is the second, which would abolish the party primary as a means of choosing party nominees. So I want to emphasize that point. It is high time we recognize that the party primary is the great "democratic reform" of the beginning of the century that failed. Indeed, many of the other tragically "democratic" reforms of that period have also failed or achieved only mixed results, but none as conspicuously as the direct primary.

In my view, the party primary is the main source of the superexpensive, superindividualistic tendencies in our politics. It creates unnecessary conflict as aspirants in the same party manufacture the most trivial, personal, and irrelevant issues to have something to slug their party colleagues with. The party primary is hypocritical, as aspirants who have been insulting and demeaning one another during the primary and may still hate one another go through a show of reconciliation and harmony on primary night, then often continue to oppose one another.

The party primary is enormously expensive, as aspirants reach out on their own to seek voters, who then fail to show up in the primary ballot booths in very great numbers. It cuts party organization and leadership completely out of the candidate selection process. That is what parties should be all about: choosing candidates.

Above all, party primaries breed division within the party and hence impede parties from performing their most important function—that is, promoting teamwork and overcoming gridlock when they gain control of government.

Representative Leach found the Burns proposal to be "a very nostalgic academic recommendation" that was "thoroughly uncompelling." In today's political atmosphere, he argued, "a synonym for strong political parties is narrow political parties." And parties should "remain broad based to be responsive to a wide variety of views." Leach continued:

For some reason the term "strong political parties" always has the implication that this is somehow positive. And I suggest as strongly as I can that that may not be the case.

To eliminate primaries and move to a system of convention politics would produce in the American scene not the current distinction of two rather centrist parties, one a little more liberal and one a little more conservative, but a two-party system in which one party could be defined as a political party and the other as a theocratic party.

One senses that Professor Burns not only prefers a parliamentary system but nostalgically has a preference for the British Conservative and Labour party model. The problem is that empowering political conventions and newer versions of cigar-smoking powerbrokers operating in backrooms today might cause the Democrats to look more like British Labourites—an unfortunate regression in my judgment—but it would not come close to making Republicans look like British Conservatives. The British Conservative model might be preferable to modern Republicanism, but empowering a powerful few at conventions instead of a larger number of individuals in primaries is not likely to produce a party characterized by Oxfordian tolerance.

Whether one likes it or not, Americans are finding political party organization increasingly irrelevant to their lives. Leadership in organizations without widespread public inter-

ests is leadership by default. On the Democratic side, it is generally leadership of activists from the union and education community; on the Republican side, increasingly from those committed to the values or organizational drive of particularist
churches.

The reform that really matters is to move in the direction of
open primaries. In states where a voter has to be registered with
a party to vote in its primary, many young people today are registering "no party." That eliminates them from the primary
process. I think that is nuts. Open primaries, in contrast, allow
people to change in each election between the Republican and
Democratic parties as they see fit, so that they can participate in
the primary process. That strengthens the parties by broadening
them.

In addition, the concept of strong political parties implies
that elected representatives should adhere to political party pre-
cepts, which means narrowing their own judgment. That does
not fit America at all, and particularly does not fit an America
that is broadening with many new and differing kinds of interests in the body politic. We ought to have legislators who
respond to conscience in the Burkian sense, which means legislators with a broader perspective rather than a narrower one.

The biggest problem, though, is quality. Throughout
American society, particularly in business, everyone is talking
about quality control. It has not been applied, however, to government. We need stronger people, not stronger parties, and the
real danger is that stronger parties mean weaker people and
narrower agendas. It is only by widening the base of the parties,
widening participation in the primary process, that we have
any hope of having stronger people and a wider panoply of
views reflected.

*White House correspondent Andrea Mitchell concurred with
Representative Leach:*

I have a slightly jaundiced view about political parties
because I began my reporting career in the city of Philadelphia,
covering the Democratic machine, which after years of

Republican rule was in firm control of all levels of every ward, every precinct, and every city office from zoning and tax collecting to law enforcement and the mayor's office. And a decade or so of covering Pennsylvania and Philadelphia politics left me with a deeply inbred suspicion of political parties. In my experience political parties have been antidemocratic and have not fostered what we would hope to be greater participation in our democracy.

Intervening from the audience, Daniel Schorr of National Public Radio supported Professor Burns's "radical proposals" but thought them "not quite radical enough." He suggested an addition:

For the parties to disburse money to candidates would be on the whole a good thing, but more important than money today in a political campaign is television time. I would like to see parties enabled to disburse television time as well. That would require that television campaigning be all done on time freely donated by networks and television stations—which would be a small payment for the gold mines they have been handed under a promise that they would perform in the public interest, convenience, and necessity—in such a way that it would not be misused by one candidate or another in a position to speak over the heads of parties. I think parties have been in a process of downgrading for a long time not only because they do not control the money that candidates can raise but because they do not control access to television.

This proposal prompted more misgivings from Representative Leach:

You have to ask who it is that will make these allocations? I would strongly warn everybody that leadership of the political parties is leadership by default. Anyone who has a desire to go to a meeting—and today in the Republican party it is increasingly one kind of group—can suddenly take over that party with great ease. That process has very little to do with reflecting in a democratic way things that are of great meaning to the vast majority of people.

So, who is going to make these allocations? Is it going to be the kind of leadership that is likely to come to the fore five or ten years from now? My personal fear is that the kind of parties that are likely to emerge will not have the kind of leadership you would want to posit with new powers of the nature being suggested.

Burns offered his rebuttal to the Leach argument:

It is very easy to talk about corruption, incompetence, inefficiency, bad representation, and nonparticipation in our present political parties. This is our point, that the party system has declined to where you can come in quite properly and honestly and say, "Here are the problems." The question, it seems to me, is not so much the quality of the present parties as it is the capacity of the parties to be regenerated, to return to the role that they once had but cleansed of their corruption.

So, those of us who advocate restoring and utilizing the parties are talking about party reforms that would, we hope, deal with the very problems of party leadership, honesty, representation, and the like that have been raised. We have a model—particularly the British model, but one that exists throughout the Western world and elsewhere as well. That model, which nobody says is free of failings, is of two very broad, very participatory parties, but parties that are not based on tremendous numbers of people coming into the nominating process. Smaller but representative groups come together to make the most crucial decisions that face any party, the selection of its candidates.

The two broad, participatory parties then wage their battle. One wins—in our case the presidency—and does its thing. After a while, the other party will improve itself and make a comeback. So, the great pendulum of politics moves back and forth. That is the model.

Today this model is failing, which calls for major analysis on our part. Can the parties be regenerated? What would have to be done? How could it be done? How promising is that route if we invest resources in it as against investing them in trying to get constitutional change? With the constitutional amendment process the Framers gave us, I suggest that we can make changes in the party constitutions much more readily than we can amend the U.S. Constitution.

Yet I must end by saying with a sinking heart, I fear that the parties have come into such bad repute, as many have said, that it is impossible to regenerate them. In that case many who might fear major institutional change are going to have to make some tough decisions as to where they stand. They are going to have to say, "If we cannot do this through party regeneration, we are going to have to do it, if something has to be done, through restructuring the American political system."

Donald Robinson, the CCS research director, challenged Burns's thesis that, because amending the Constitution is so difficult, reforming the parties offers a more feasible course for those seeking structural improvement in the government:

Assuming that a year from now Clinton has not produced a successful reform of public policy, what should we be doing about that? What reforms are necessary? The party reformers argue that constitutional reform is impossible and therefore we should be attending to strengthening the parties.

I doubt that party reform is any more possible than constitutional reform. Parties are held in very low regard in our country. I understand all the arguments for parties' being essential to democracy, but there is going to be no public opinion support for reforms to strengthen parties, such as giving parties a lot of public funds to spend.

There are a number of reasons that political parties have been historically fragmented and weak in America. One of the major reasons is the constitutional environment, which fragments parties. If we want effective, accountable governance, we have to attend to constitutional factors, to simplify our form of government and make it a better vehicle of effectiveness and accountability. The people will not support stronger parties, which is why I prefer to talk about constitutional reform.

4 Congressional Reform

Barbara Sinclair, professor of political science at the University of California, presented a paper on reform of the House of Representatives that concluded, surprisingly to some, that the House does not need further major structural change:

First, what is it we want Congress to do? Obviously, we expect Congress to represent: to bring into the legislative process the views, needs, desires of its members' constituents, and to provide a forum where the full range of views is expressed. We also expect Congress to make decisions, to pass laws.

But clearly not just any laws will do. Here, two criteria are frequently mentioned: Congress should pass laws that reflect the will of the people, that respond to popular majorities. And Congress should pass laws that deal promptly and effectively with pressing national problems. But these two criteria, which can be labeled responsiveness and responsibility, are distinct and sometimes contradictory. Only in a perfect world would what the majority wants always accord with what policy experts think is likely to be most effective.

In recent years, much elite discourse has assumed that when a conflict exists, responsibility should take priority—in other words, do what is right rather than what is popular. But if Congress regularly thwarts popular majorities, it loses in legitimacy. And honest, well-meaning people, including members of Congress, are not necessarily going to agree on what is right. So, to some extent tension will always exist between responsiveness and responsibility.

In terms of institutional design, the requisites of representation and those of lawmaking are different. A decentralized, open, permeable body in which individual members have considerable resources and autonomy of action has great potential for articulating the broad variety of opinions and interests in our society. A more centralized, hierarchical body is more capable of expeditious decisionmaking. In terms of process, representation takes time, especially when there are a great variety of viewpoints; by definition, lawmaking requires closure, an end to debate, and, implicitly or explicitly, a choice among competing alternatives. In most circumstances, an acceptable balance can be struck between the demands of representation and those of lawmaking, but it is essential to remember that the values cannot be maximized simultaneously.

The most prevalent diagnosis of what is wrong with the House is that it is too decentralized and too entrepreneurial, a body incapable and unwilling to be led, in which party is all but irrelevant. But as a description of the contemporary House, that is off the mark in key respects. The House of the 1980s and early 1990s is not nearly as decentralized or as resistant to central leadership as that model depicts. During the 1980s, House Democrats became markedly more cohesive in their voting behavior and their party leadership became more active and more consequential in the legislative process.

The reforms of the 1970s, which are usually described as decentralizing reforms, also enhanced the powers of the party leadership and reduced those of committee chairs. In the adversarial political climate of the 1980s, Democrats found that they really needed leadership help to pass legislation that they considered at all acceptable, and so they became more willing to let their leaders use aggressively the powers that they had been given. The leaders have significant resources in a very active whip system and, most important of all, real control over the Rules Committee. In short, the current system in the House offers a much better solution to the dilemmas of organizational design than the committee-government system of the prereform House.

If things are not really so bad, then why gridlock? The short answer is mostly divided government. When control is divided and the parties strongly disagree on policy, then having a reasonably homogeneous and reasonably strongly led majority party in Congress actually increases the chances of stalemate.

Under such circumstances, the president is less able to break off enough majority party members to pass his own proposals. In other words, a Republican president cannot depend on the conservative coalition anymore, and yet the president, because he possesses the veto, can usually thwart the majority party's efforts at significant policy innovation. Obviously, hard choices do not become easy when one party controls both the presidency and the Congress, but the differences are likely to be less fundamental and, crucially, blame for not dealing with the problems is much harder to dissipate.

Is this then an argument for the status quo? It is an argument against attempting comprehensive internal change. A thorough organizational overhaul is not needed. With so little agreement among members about either the need for or the contours of a comprehensive internal overhaul, the prospects for such change are dim in any case. The current opportunity can best be used to make some more limited but nonetheless important changes in internal functioning and a major change in an area where more consensus for its necessity exists: campaign finance reform.

Professor Sinclair outlined her recommendations for changes in organization and procedures of the House:

I make no attempt to be comprehensive in topics covered or to discuss them in detail. Thomas Mann and Norman Ornstein, in *Renewing Congress: A First Report*, have made an impressive beginning at drawing up a broad-ranging agenda for possible reforms.

Responsible lawmaking requires a plan: an agenda or list of priorities and a schedule for enactment. The House majority party has lacked a process for coming up with a meaningful party agenda when it does not control the White House. At its December meetings, the Democratic caucus created a new party committee, chosen by the Speaker and consisting of rank-and-file members and committee chairmen, to set an agenda and to oversee its enactment. Such a committee might seem unnecessary now that Democrats hold the White House; certainly

Clinton will, like presidents before him, set the agenda for his party. Still, by having a formal process within the party for determining members' preferences as to priorities, House Democrats' preferences may well carry more weight with Clinton. And, to the extent the committee can oversee the legislative process on the agenda, keeping it on schedule and on track substantively, it will contribute enormously to the party's success.

Keeping priority legislation moving on schedule will depend upon the Speaker's willingness to use his referral powers and his ability to set deadlines for committees and sometimes perhaps on his use of the ad hoc committee device. With the agenda now bearing the direct imprimatur of the caucus, the Speaker should be willing to use those powers expansively.

The budget process should be reexamined with the objective of possibly streamlining the process. With the relaxation of tensions between the legislative and executive branches, now is the time to experiment. A two-year budget resolution and perhaps a revised entity to draft it are worth trying out.

Jurisdictional battles among committees have become a problem of some significance in the House, and recently turf wars seem to have been a greater threat than policy differences to the timely reporting of legislation. Realigning committee jurisdictions so as to eliminate overlap is impossible in a world where problems are complex and multifaceted, and multiple referral is a reasonable solution. Still, the way the process works now is far from ideal. At minimum, some tidying up of jurisdictions should be undertaken, the extent of the jurisdictional claim needed for a referral should be increased, and referral only for study warrants serious consideration.

The proliferation of select committees and of subcommittees has frequently been criticized, but the activity of these units, which consists mostly of holding hearings, is not, I would argue, a problem. By publicizing problems, airing issues, and promoting possible policy solutions, they perform useful functions. To the extent that they give junior members means of participating, that is all to the good. However, to the extent that they take up members' time at the expense of their directly legislative duties on their standing committees, a real problem does exist. Still, that problem might be more effectively addressed directly rather than by the abolition of competing units.

As House Democrats began getting their act together in the 1980s, House Republicans became more and more unhappy with their position and role in the chamber. Changes should be considered that would lessen the minority's dissatisfaction without, however, making the majority less capable of legislating.

Specifically, limiting the majority party leadership's use of restrictive rules would be a major mistake. Through the use of restrictive rules, debate can be focused on the major alternatives, compromises can be protected from being picked apart on the floor, and floor time can be apportioned in a reasonably sensible way. The minority should, of course, continue to be allowed to offer its alternative version of legislation brought to the floor by the majority.

Professor Sinclair reserved her greatest emphasis for the issue of campaign finance reform:

If the Congress can seldom expect to be popular, that makes it all the more important that it not be perceived as venal. The widespread perception that Congress is dominated by special interest groups has as much potential as continuing gridlock to undermine Congress's legitimacy. The perception can itself contribute to gridlock; a Congress the public believes is bought will have much less leeway to make hard choices.

Many people attribute gridlock in considerable part to the influence of special interests. Although I believe that argument is overblown and that genuine policy differences between the president and the congressional majority were much more important, a very real problem exists—even if only a problem of perceptions. And the only feasible solution is campaign finance reform with a considerable component, direct or indirect, of public financing.

Attempts to restrict lobbying quickly run up against First Amendment problems. In any case, much lobbying is useful:

members need the technical and the political information conveyed. Elections are blunt instruments for conveying voters' policy preferences. It is not lobbying itself but the perception that groups buy votes—almost certainly not true—and access—very frequently true—by campaign contributions that is so pernicious. And the only way to combat that perception is to lessen the influence of "interested" money in campaigns.

Among congressional scholars there is near universal agreement that campaign finance reform is essential and should be the first priority of reform. The guidelines laid out in the Mann-Ornstein report represent, to a large extent, a consensus of the scholarly community.

Several other speakers also appealed for campaign finance reform. Andrea Mitchell saw it as "the real solution" to the problems under discussion:

If we do not come to grips with campaign finance reform, we will never see the proliferation of better ideas in Washington that we all hoped would begin with the large influx of newcomers in the Congress. I think we in the media need to keep the pressure on if campaign finance reform is not to become just another campaign promise that falls by the wayside, because some in Congress argue that it should not apply to the 1994 election cycle, and some in the White House believe that their economic concerns are predominant and are not willing to take on another fight with Congress at a time when they have to invest so much in getting the economic package passed.

Representative Leach advocated going "very, very far in campaign reform":

I personally object to Common Cause for not being radical enough. A far greater problem than gridlock is the problem that one political party has had a padlock on the legislative process in Washington, and that means a padlock on reform. And how many of you have heard Democrat after Democrat say they support campaign reform, and yet it has never appeared, for the very self-evident reason that the current system ensconces the status quo—the status quo in which one political party has dominated the United States House of Representatives for forty years. And that is a greater problem—if one thinks that the legislature should reflect shifts in the public mood and be accountable—than any gridlock that may occur between the executive and legislative branches of government.

Mitchell noted that the blame should be shared by both parties. Despite the "initial reluctance of the Democrats to come to grips with it," she said, "at least we could have had some improvements had it not been blocked by the White House and the Republicans in the Senate."

Howard Paster gave assurance that while campaign finance reform was unquestionably a difficult issue among Democrats, it "is not something that the president will need any media pressure to stay on. The president convened a meeting in the Cabinet Room with leading Hill Democrats on this issue two weeks after taking the oath. It is an issue he will stay on and he will succeed on."

Former Representative Thomas Downey advocated campaign finance reform and "tinkering at the margin" with House rules and practices, but expected little genuine improvement unless public attitudes changed, because the Congress reflects its constituency:

Americans have no great appreciation for the majesty of their history, no real, detailed understanding of the great issues that face us as a people, and no willingness to sacrifice and look at the long term. Far too many of our citizens, if they will not say it directly, in fact embrace the idea expressed in a recent movie that greed is good. Now given these national shortcomings, what can we expect from the men and women who inhabit the Congress? Most members, especially in the House, are great mirrors of their constituency.

Some of my former colleagues say, "Do nothing, do not worry, things are okay. We have a Democratic president and there is really not much that we have to do now. Now that we have eliminated divided government we will have eliminated gridlock." They are wrong, as are those who say term limitations, balanced budget amendments, line item vetoes, are what we need.

There are some things that we need to tinker with that will make the institution a bit more responsive to the broader needs of our country, but even after we have done them, if we do not have good citizens, we will still not have a good Congress.

Campaign finance reform is a good idea as long as you do not, in the process of reform, turn members of Congress into full-time as opposed to part-time campaign fundraisers. So how do you deal with it? In a way broadly similar to what the House has approved in the past: some limitations on contributions and spending and some public financing. But do not hold out a great deal of hope that this by itself is going to make a great deal of difference. It will not.

Another improvement would be, at least in the House, to try the Oxford Union debate format, where the parties designate their champions to sally forth, so that we would have structured debates instead of the mind-numbing drivel that normally occurs during special orders at the end of the day. People who are addicted to C-SPAN would actually hear something worth listening to.

These suggestions are, to be sure, tinkering at the margins. They are the sort of tinkering that will make the institutions better, make them more satisfying for the public and for the members of Congress, but we need to deal with some deeper and more insidious problems in our country before we improve our Congress.

In contrast to Professor Sinclair's diagnosis of the House as basically healthy, Steven Smith, professor of political science at the University of Minnesota, saw the Senate as in need of "radical surgery":

The Senate has come to a place where it is now failing to live up to its traditional role. Really radical surgery, judged by

Senate standards, is required to preserve its role. Two issues dominate recent discussion.

First, are the talents of the one hundred senators being put to good use? The answer is that the talents of senators are often squandered on activities that do not contribute to the general welfare either of their individual states or of the nation, and the quality of public policy is one victim.

Second, should Senate minorities be allowed to delay or obstruct action beyond the delay and stalemate that comes with the separation-of-powers, bicameral system created by the Constitution?

Squandered talent and obstructionism are the product of two forces: the rules and practices inherited from the past, and important changes in the political context of Senate activity during recent decades. The combination has produced a dysfunctional Senate, one sorely in need of change.

Let me begin by quoting Harvard's first Ph.D. in political science, Henry Cabot Lodge, who was elected to the Senate one hundred years ago. He said, "Under these century-old rules for which there is often a fine disregard, the Senate still transacts its business largely by unanimous consent and with the consideration for the wishes and convenience of each senator, very agreeable to them although not a little laughed at by an irreverent public." He added, "To vote without debating is perilous, but to debate and never vote is imbecile. A body which cannot govern itself will not long hold the respect of the people who have chosen it to govern the country."

For some commentators, the freedom of debate allowed the Senate to become a great deliberative body. Many observers cite the great traditions started by the debates among Daniel Webster, Henry Clay, John C. Calhoun, and others in the decades preceding the Civil War. But Webster and Clay were among the most prominent sponsors of proposals to limit Senate debate.

As we all know, the current rule allows three-fifths of all duly elected senators—sixty if they are all present—to invoke cloture, except that two-thirds of those present and voting are required to invoke cloture on any matter affecting the Senate's rules. Besides producing delay, diluting public policy, and sometimes killing vital legislation, the rule has had disastrous effects on everyday practices in the Senate, particularly those relating to unanimous consent and what are called "holds."

In the modern Senate, the majority leader seeks unanimous consent to bring a bill to the floor and often seeks to limit or structure debate and amendments by unanimous consent, because the Senate lacks a general rule limiting debate and amendments, except for the cumbersome cloture rule. But the leader's dependence on unanimous consent means that any senator can upset his plans. Consequently, the majority leader consults with the minority leader—a nice feature of Senate politics—and other interested senators before seeking consent on all but the most routine questions. In recent decades, this process of soliciting and recording possible objections has become institutionalized. Well-understood routines are in place for senators to register objections, reservations, and concerns about requests to take up bills, nominations, and even treaties. The registered objections are known as holds, reflecting their potential effect on legislation.

These Senate rules and practices have not always posed a big problem for Senate leaders. As recently as the early 1960s, senators did not pursue or threaten filibusters with much frequency. And with little real threat of a filibuster to back it up, senators did not use holds with much frequency or effectiveness. But conditions have changed.

This is illustrated by the dramatic increase in filibusters and in the number of cloture motions. Majority Leader George Mitchell has pointed out that the 1919–70 period saw a total of 50 cloture votes, not quite one a year. The 1971–92 period saw 295 cloture votes, more than 13 a year. The last two years, 1991–92, set a record with 48 cloture votes.

Obstructionism has become even more objectionable as the filibusters have been applied to the motion to proceed, even to take up legislation on the Senate floor. From 1977 through 1982, only six cloture votes were held on the motion to proceed, but in 1991 and 1992, there were thirty-five cloture votes on that form of motion alone. Poor George Mitchell, in the last two years, has had to pursue a unanimous consent agreement that limited debate or amendments in some way for about one of every three measures that have come to the Senate floor. That is five times the frequency of 1959–60, when Lyndon Johnson was majority leader.

One result of this tremendous change is a regular lecture by the majority leader to his colleagues, usually futile, about not abusing their individual rights. But depending on the leader's assertiveness and appeals to colleagues to resist temptation—or perhaps insisting on a more aggressive leader—will not be enough to change current practice, given the strength of the incentives for individual senators to exploit their position. Something more radical, more institutional, is required to alter the incentives for senators.

The agenda for reforming the Senate is not new. I support campaign finance reform, sharply reducing and reorganizing committees and staff, and biennial budgeting. We should also move to realign the election schedule. Now the House and Senate are really on an eighteen-month, not a two-year election cycle, because the first congressional primaries pop up in the winter and then they stretch out all the way until October. Forcing every congressional primary to be held after Labor Day would shorten the general election campaign and reserve as much of the two-year term for legislating as possible. A case can also be made for peeling back some of the sunshine rules. There is no reason why every meeting has to be held in public, unless a majority of the members vote otherwise. Current rules encourage members to negotiate details in private so as not to make fools of themselves in public and to turn over responsibility to staff and exclude members from negotiations.

But nothing matters in the Senate as much as the absence of general rules and precedents limiting debate and amendments on the floor. A leader's ability to manage the Senate schedule is limited by the absence of such rules. Deliberative activities on and off the Senate floor are undermined by the stop-and-go character of Senate activity. And holds, another obstructionist technique, gain their bite from the absence of general rules limiting debate and amendments. Needless to say, there are obstacles to changing the cloture rule, because any change can be fili-bustered and a two-thirds vote is required to overcome that fili-buster. But the Senate has not engaged in creative thinking about its basic rules, and the time has come for it to do so.

I propose that the Senate create a committee of the whole for Senate floor action. The Senate would move into the com-mittee of the whole upon the adoption of a nondebatable motion, offered by the majority leader or his designee, that is approved by a simple majority. When in committee of the whole, the Senate would conduct general debate, fixed by rule (say, one hour to each side), consider legislation for amendment by title, allow only germane amendments, limit debate on amendments (say, one hour to each side), and limit debate on debatable procedural motions, points of order, or appeals to thirty minutes or less. In committee of the whole, the Senate could further restrict debate or amendments by majority vote. On a nondebatable motion, subject to majority approval, the Senate could rise from the committee of the whole.

Before or after the Senate considered legislation within the committee of the whole, the current rules would apply (that is, on most matters limits on debate and amendments outside the committee of the whole could be applied only by unanimous consent or invoking cloture). In this way, senators' current rights would be preserved and yet most debate on legislation would occur in a more controlled and predictable setting. Nothing would prevent cloture from being invoked before or after the consideration of legislation in the committee of the whole.

In the current situation, the biggest obstacle seems to be Robert Byrd. Many senators believe that he has a monopoly on expertise, and good thought, and understanding about the Senate rules. It is not so.

Procedural changes are usually described as having only a marginal effect on policy outcomes. Leaders and outside observers generally give them little priority. And at any given time on any one issue that is undeniable. Yet the procedural set-ting has a pervasive effect in most political institutions, includ-ing the Senate. It influences whether members spend time with each other and how they do so. It greatly influences the character of constituency and interest group pressures and how members respond to them.

The Senate has simply reached a point at which its basic procedures, interacting with a rapidly changing and irresistible political environment, undermine its special policymaking functions. Now is the time to insist that the Senate act to reform itself.

Former Senator Warren Rudman categorically disputed Professor Smith's analysis and recommendations:

Let me say quite frankly that I disagree with about everything I have heard in the last half hour. Those who make the art of political science their pursuit tend to delve very heavily into structure, form, and organization—things which really have nothing to do with the problems facing the Senate and the House, because the gridlock that we speak of is not so much between the Congress and the president but between the government and its people, who have a totally erroneous perception of what the government is and what it does. A *Washington Post* poll, for instance, found that about 70 percent of the American people believed that a full 50 percent of government expenditures were waste, fraud, and abuse. And about 75 percent agreed on a solution. You could eliminate the deficit by eliminating waste, fraud, and abuse, and foreign aid—which that year was one-and-one half percent of the federal budget—and, of course, congressional perks.

Here is a number for you: Americans with incomes of better than $50,000 a year receive $150 billion annually in entitlements from the federal government of all types. But members of Congress cannot deal with that kind of a situation, with a constituency that does not want to listen to what the problem is, and a press that has not been terribly helpful until the last eighteen months. You can talk about reforming the rules and the committee system, and campaign finance and all the rest, but until the American people have some understanding of what their government does and how it does it, and are willing to make changes, nothing will happen, because the members are concerned with reelection and survival.

So, what is the problem with Congress? First, the whole country has become experts. The talk show hosts get going on a subject and by ten o'clock that night every American who listens to those shows knows more than the most senior staffer of the appropriate committee in the Congress. Read my mail for the last year and you will find out. They just know. And if you try to tell them to the contrary, they do not want to listen. And the American public has not been told the truth for a long time by its political leadership of either party. Net result, gridlock. Gridlock in what way? Gridlock in being unable to cast votes that put the caster of those votes in political jeopardy.

We have to have a president and a Congress and people in the private sector—be it Ross Perot, the Concord Coalition, or whoever—willing to get engaged in bringing to the American people the truth about what we are facing. And then, whether greed or reason will triumph, at least the outcome will be based on understanding, not ignorance.

As for the filibuster rule, during my twelve years in the Senate, I saw it used a great deal, yet on very important legislation that was truly in the national interest, eventually something was worked out. By and large, major legislation did pass.

Many times, though, some of us would go privately to the leadership and say, "For God's sake, put their feet to the fire." Tell them, "If you want to put a hold on the assistant secretary for Pakistan affairs because his brother-in-law did not support you in your campaign, fine. Go out on the floor and talk about that for three days. You want to make a damned fool of yourself? Good luck."

The leaders never did it, but if they put senators' feet to the fire they would not have to worry about Rule 22. It would work only when in fact it ought to work, never in all those ways that people have made it work as a threat. Let the leadership put people to the test and then watch them fold because they are being watched and look like fools to people in their own states.

Professor Smith responded:

They did not fold when Senator Byrd as majority leader held their feet to the fire on campaign finance reform a few years ago, and eventually only he was worn out.

The Senate has given in on budget matters. On reconciliation bills, it holds itself to time limits and prohibits nongermane amendments. It was only in conditions of crisis, during the budget agreements of 1985 and 1990, that it finally agreed to those limits, but in any case senators themselves have occasionally agreed that the rules are a problem. My feeling is that what is good enough for the budget is good enough for civil rights, or gun control, or anything else.

The problem for Clinton, then, will not be in getting his budget cuts through in the form of a reconciliation bill. His problem will come with the health care bill, which will not be protected by time limits or limits on amendments.

The filibuster, and the ability of a large minority to block legislation in the Senate, certainly were not anticipated in the Constitution. The preservation of liberty was structured by requiring three branches of government—the House, the Senate, and the president—to agree before legislation could get passed. The argument that an additional Senate rule is needed to preserve minority rights requires extraordinary justification. Actually, the current rule exists largely by reason of historical accident.

What we are facing here is a bald political calculation on the part of any minority. Democrats defended Rule 22 when Republican presidents were in the White House in order to block their legislation. That is really why Rule 22 has been maintained all these years—because of bald political calculation, not because of any serious fundamental philosophy about minority rights in the Senate.

Former Representative Downey endorsed the proposal for a national primary, but would extend it to cover the presidency as well as the Congress:

I love Professor Smith's idea of a national primary, held in September. This is a good idea if just for the internal operations of the House, because the first primary occurs in Illinois and others are staggered throughout the rest of the election year. You know you are not going to have to work Monday because Monday comes right after Sunday, when everyone is home. And so, if a primary election is held on Tuesday, there is no reason to come in on that day either. And the Wednesday session cannot start until one or two o'clock in the House. So, a national primary—and I would apply it also to the presidency and the Senate—could make things more efficient.

5 Constitutional Reform

*D**onald Robinson opened the discussion of constitutional reform with a paper entitled "The Problem Is Constitutional," using the 1987 report of the Committee on the Constitutional System as his initial point of reference:*

In analyzing the performance of the American constitutional system on the occasion of its bicentennial in 1987, the Committee on the Constitutional System identified three "unmistakable . . . signs of strain":

—the mounting national debt, fueled anew each year by huge deficits that "defy the good intentions of legislators and presidents";

—the inconsistency of our foreign and national security policies, with president and Congress often operating at cross-purposes, tempting presidents to launch important diplomatic, military, and covert activities in secret and without consulting Congress; and

—malfunctions in the electoral system, including the high cost and stupefying length of campaigns, and persistently low turnout rates.

The committee traced these problems, complex as they were, to a common cause: the "diffuse structure of the executive-legislative process" and the inability of modern American political parties to bridge the constitutional gaps.

At the core of the CCS program has been a desire to forge closer ties between the executive and legislative branches, whether by strengthening political parties or by revising the constitutional incentives away from conflict and confrontation and toward greater cooperation. Some members have looked with admiration upon the ability of parliamentary systems to "form a government," to enact and implement a coherent set of policies, and to be held accountable by the electorate for the results. They have wondered whether we might adapt some features of the parliamentary model to our own needs. Thus, the CCS has suggested repealing the constitutional bar against members of Congress serving in the administration without giving up their seats in Congress; coordinating the electoral cycles of legislators and executives; and adopting straight party tickets, to improve the chance that both branches would be controlled by the same party. The animating purpose of these proposals is twofold: to strengthen governance and to make it more accountable.

In recent years, conventional opinion has begun to focus on "divided government" as a principal cause of the mess in Washington: the scandals—HUD, savings and loan, Iran-contra—but above all, the failure of the government to encourage economic growth and provide adequate health care coverage. Exit polls taken on Election Day 1992, for example, showed that voters were finally beginning to see a connection between divided government and poor governmental performance. Fully two-thirds of those who voted for Bill Clinton or George Bush for president thought that the government would work better if both president and Congress were controlled by the same party; even Perot voters agreed, by a 48 to 41 percent margin.

There is no reason to think, however, that the public is ready to adopt the remedies offered by the CCS to correct divided government, such as public financing of campaigns through the parties, or mandatory straight tickets. In fact, in the last few years, debate over the CCS program, and the ideas of structural reformers in general, began to be drowned out by a reform impulse of a quite different character. The leading candidate of this new wave of institutional reformers seemed to be term limitations, a proposal born of a desire to loosen the grip of entrenched incumbents, who were blamed for such outrages as the congressional banking and post office scandals. Similar populist impulses are fueling the drive for campaign finance reform, to put ceilings on spending and reduce the corrupting influence of political action committees.

The positive side of this sentiment found expression in the presidential campaign of H. Ross Perot, who promised to use modern communications technology to link the people more directly to their government. Perot, with his on-again, off-again campaign, and with a vice-presidential nominee whose lack of qualifications revealed the appalling shallowness of Perot's movement, nevertheless won almost 19 percent of the vote. His bottomless pockets doubtless helped, but it was an impressive performance nonetheless, and it provided a measure of the frustration felt last year by many citizens toward the government in Washington.

Thus the agenda of reform presents a bewildering picture. On the one hand, many people in Washington sense that government is ineffective and perhaps excessively checked. They argue that, for the sake of effectiveness and to make electoral accountability possible, the government needs to be empowered and liberated from a constitutional structure designed for another age. On the other hand, people outside Washington sense that the government is out of touch, that its agendas and actions are controlled by men and women who are somehow insulated from the concerns of common people. They are not about to strengthen a structure that serves such alien purposes.

If this analysis is correct, we must find a way to strengthen government, but at the same time make it more democratic, more consistently accountable to the people from whom it draws its strength. The lesson of our nation's experience is that you cannot strengthen government in America without making it more democratic.

The Framers of 1787 understood this. By making the House of Representatives directly elected and an equal partner in government, and by making the president as nearly directly elected as the existence of slavery would permit, the Framers were able to gain ratification for a system much stronger than the pre-existing form. Amendments over the ensuing century have made it ever more inclusive and democratic. Blacks and women and eighteen-year-olds gained the vote, the Senate joined the House and president in being directly elected, and supposed constitutional obstacles to positive governance were gradually interpreted out of existence by the Supreme Court. There remains a great deal of vitality to the notion of state and local responsibility for important aspects of governance, but people look to the federal government without hesitation now for the solution to problems that require national approaches.

Finally, a few words about our immediate predicament. We are currently in the midst of our regular, quadrennial renewal of spirit, sometimes called the "honeymoon," wherein a new president, having received a fresh mandate from the electorate, sets out to solve our problems. Like innocents, we give ourselves to the illusion that things will be different this time.

I am one of those people who hope that we have gotten the right combination: a man in the White House who understands the need for candid consultation with Congress, and who has the skill, intelligence, stamina, and self-confidence to make this system work. I am immensely reassured, for example, by the time he and the vice president—and, yes, their wives—are taking to consult with the leadership in Congress about key elements in their legislative program. I am reassured as well by their apparent determination to insist on multilateral approaches to conflicts in Europe and Africa. These are positive signs.

Yet we must remind ourselves of some enduring realities. One is that, as Lord Bryce put it in a related context, "success in a lottery" does not justify trusting our fate to chance. This time, we appear to have elected a pair of unusually skillful and resourceful politicians to lead the executive branch. It has not always been so, and it will not be in the future. Remember, too, that President Bush began his term in a similar atmosphere of euphoria, full of smart, deadlock-breaking deals with Congress. It was not long before the two branches were at one another's throat over the budget, and the bitter taste of that struggle set teeth on edge for the balance of Mr. Bush's term in office. Constitutions must be designed for the long haul, for good times and bad, and for incompetent leaders as well as those with special skills.

Trouble is bound to come, because our system is cannily built to ensure it. For, as Madison wrote in *The Federalist*, each branch in our constitutional system has "a will of its own," and each official has "the necessary constitutional means and personal motives" to defend his or her own political and constitutional turf. Sooner or later, issues will arise that divide people in such a way as to make governance virtually impossible. In the absence of strong parties, that moment is likely to come sooner rather than later. And what is worse, in the absence of strong parties, it will be impossible to tell who is responsible for the paralysis. Public opinion will be a muddle, because government is a muddle.

We need to modify this system of incentives. We need to provide "constitutional means and personal motives" to encourage cooperation between the branches, so that platforms can be enacted and implemented and the government held accountable for the results at the ensuing election. That will require a radical simplification of the structure and a mechanism for taking the government to the nation whenever it breaks down or needs a fresh mandate.

I should make it clear that I do not speak for the CCS. The approach of that group has always been far more cautious, less radical, than mine. But my appraisal is that we need more coherent, more effective, more accountable government. I do not know whether we are likely to get it soon, nor whether we will have it by "reflection and choice." If a crisis comes quickly, and we are unprepared, we are likely to be the victims of "accident and force" and end up with government far worse than what we have now.

James Sundquist expanded on various reform proposals discussed by the Committee on the Constitutional System and urged that the Congress create a commission to examine the need for fundamental constitutional change:

Even if we can be optimistic about the short term—the next four years, or maybe eight—we have to look at the long term, which is what the Committee on the Constitutional System has been trying to do. And when you look at the long term, you know that one election that produces unified government, such as that of 1992, by no means brings any final solution to the problem of divided government.

In the years ahead, the Republicans are likely to elect the president half the time, just by the law of averages or maybe better than that. Since the Democrats will probably continue to control the House all of the time, the government will still be divided half of the time. And if divided government is as bad as many have been saying that it is, we still have to deal with that problem. Somehow we have to find a way through revising our electoral system—which takes us back to the Constitution—to make divided government less likely.

One question that the CCS was able to agree on almost unanimously concerned the length of the term for members of the House of Representatives: two years is simply too short. Members do not have time to get settled before they are running again and going out to raise money from the political action committees. They have no breathing space in which to do what they campaigned to do before they have to face the voters again. They need a period of time free from imminent voter retribution to do those tough things that have to be done. No other country in the world has a term as short as two years for its legislative body. It is almost an article of faith in Washington that the window of opportunity to get things done for a new president is about six months. After that, everybody is thinking about the next election and running for cover, and in the midterm election the president always gets a setback and then everybody waits in the hope that the next presidential election will straighten things out. Terms of four years for representatives and eight years for senators, as the CCS recommended, would eliminate the midterm election and give everyone a longer time horizon.

Another reform that the committee talked about a great deal is the need in our system for a safety valve when the government palpably breaks down, for whatever reason. We need a system for dissolving the government and holding special elections to get a fresh start. Almost every other country has a way of dissolving a government that can no longer lead and govern. If the United States had such a system, it probably would not be used more than once or twice a century. But when the time comes that the government is hopelessly impotent and ineffective, we have no safety valve. One is needed.

Those are among the constitutional reforms that the CCS has been talking about for the last dozen years. The next question is, how do we get there from here? If the country ever does seriously consider the structure of our government, the first step is going to have to be, as in so many other structural and procedural reforms, a commission that can raise the discussion from the level of unofficial, self-appointed groups like the CCS to the status of an official body. That was the means used to reorganize the executive branch, going back to the Brownlow committee and the first Hoover commission. It was used in reorganizing the legislative branch with the La Follette-Monroney committee of 1946 and a whole series of later ones, including the joint committee that is working at the present time.

But the country has never had a commission that looked at the relations between the branches, the fundamental structure of the government. Maybe not now, but somewhere down the road, we will have to confront these fundamental structural questions through the initiative of some kind of official study commission on the patterns of those that have worked so effectively in dealing with the executive and legislative branches as independent entities.

James MacGregor Burns also "very strongly" favored a four-year term for the House of Representatives.

Former Representative Thomas Downey disagreed that the governmental structure is the basic problem:

To be successful, a president and a Congress have to do what Reagan did: concentrate on one thing, get one thing done at a time and use the momentum of each to help the next. It is not the structure that is going to slow down the process as much as it is the sheer burden and the size of the programs. You cannot deal with 14 or 15 percent of the gross national product in terms of health care and assume that is going to be done quickly, until you have explained it to the country and done a host of other things. The structure will help but it is much more a question of focus and political courage.

Representative Leach went further, terming it "unfitting" even to
suggest that the Constitution is unsuited to modern times:

Perspective is always difficult to apply to events of the day, and there is a penchant for emphasizing all the bad news rather than the good. But if we have any sense of history at all, the last half century has been about the success of democracy, particularly American democracy. American democracy has defeated totalitarianism of the right and the left and provided a model for many other countries. American political and economic principles have created more opportunity for people around the world as they followed our model. Why this country is in such enormous self-doubt when we should be more self-confident, I do not understand.

It strikes me that the Founding Fathers have been vindicated, and the suggestion hinted at by Professor Robinson, that the Constitution is now unfitting for the times, is itself an unfitting observation.

But I will say, if the Clinton administration does not succeed—and I personally am a bit skeptical—you are going to see some efforts for constitutional change that for most of American history would have been seen as absolutely irrational, but in terms of modern-day politics might have to be considered.

Radio and television reporter Cokie Roberts also minimized the
need for structural reforms:

I agree with my congressional colleagues here that the problems tend not to be structural but substantive. There are a couple of structural things I would play with, but they are more going back to the old ways than creating new ways. For instance, in the Senate if you made people actually perform a filibuster, it would make all the difference in the world. The fact is that filibusters are tough to carry out. And if the Senate leadership did not just wimp out every time somebody says "I am going to filibuster," and said, "Okay, go for it," that would make an enormous difference.

I would go further to say that the problems of the last several years have been the result of what the voters wanted. We have been dealing with a thing called democracy. Right now, the voters believe if they send their money to the Congress, the Congress will not use it for deficit reduction but will find some new way to spend it. And they are right. The onus is on both parties. The Democrats have not used government well and efficiently and have caused voters to believe that money will be wasted, and Republicans have cheapshoted the question of how the money is going, and implied that it has all gone for waste, fraud, and abuse.

When I go on call-in shows, people say, "Oh, just get rid of the congressional perks." And I say, "No, I will do you one better. Fire them all. Just send them all home." And they say, "Great." And I say, "And send all their staffs home, fire them all. Close down the Library of Congress, the Congressional Research Service, the whole kit and caboodle. Turn off the air conditioner, turn off the heat, everything." People are beginning to think this sounds really good. And then I point out that the deficit will be $333 billion instead of $335 billion. This is a little-known fact, and once you say it, people actually do believe you after a while.

We have had a public very distrustful of government and of the two political parties; they have thought the Republicans were too conservative and the Democrats too liberal, and they have quite consciously and conscientiously voted for gridlock because they are afraid of what government would do if it actually did act.

But I think that changed in this election, with much hesitancy, caution, and concern. In the exit polls on election day, 55 percent of the voters said they were either concerned about or frightened of a Clinton presidency at the same time that they voted for him. That may have changed since, because we do invest in our leaders a great deal of hope, but at least on election day people said with trepidation, "Things are not working in Washington. So, okay, let us try letting one party rule; as terrified as we are of the Democratic party, let us give them a shot and see if somebody can be responsible in Washington." Elections have consequences, and the greatest reform and structural change you can ever make is to hold an election and let people decide. That happened this time. People are wary of it, but they decided to put one party in control and see what happens. We will see whether at the next election they decide that they liked gridlock better.

Tom Oliphant of the Boston Globe *would give equal weight to procedure and substance:*

We should not quite so uniformly condemn our institutions. We cannot adore them, but there have been moments, and it is important to understand those moments even as we deplore the lack of more moments.

Why, for example, could things happen with such sudden massive speed in 1981, or in 1982 going the other way on taxes, or how did what could not happen in 1969 on tax reform happen in 1986, or how could this extremely complicated compromise that is unfairly maligned—to wit the budget deal of 1990—happen? Or, on the other side, how could Jimmy Carter's energy proposals get eviscerated in the Senate in 1978, or why did the efforts of moderate responsible Republicans in the Senate in 1985 to take a huge, serious bite out of the budget deficit start to succeed and then flop?

It is entirely possible for Clinton to lose his program because he cannot get a vote on it, because the centrifugal forces can prevent him from making his case politically on the floor the way he made his case rhetorically for support in his State of the Union address and in his speeches around the country in the days that followed. Or, he could lose one or more key components of his program because he did a lousy job of talking to the country, or because there is junk in his program, upon further examination, and it does not command public support and therefore does not produce pressure on Congress to support it.

Procedure can matter. Political substance can matter. The Congress today still has many unfortunate tendencies that keep questions from being posed directly, where the yeses or nos are recorded for future combat. And some things have not happened because the nature of our problems is such that the country is having trouble agreeing on a solution. We are, after all, a conservative culture that comes to major change only reluctantly, after consensus has had time to build. The problems that I see come as much from procedure as from substance, and you cannot really enjoy the delicious mess that we cover unless you give equal weight to both.

Former Senator Howard Baker, who also served as White House chief of staff, urged the delegation of more budgetary power by the Congress to the president:

The conflict, or the misunderstanding, or the friction between the White House and the Congress is the most important single conflict in our domestic political arena. Divided government may not mean a difference of parties occupying the White House and having the majority in the Congress, but may simply refer to the corrosive and sometimes destructive conflict between the two branches. That is the form of divided government that we really need to address and concern ourselves with.

When I came to the Congress in 1967, and even before that, when my father was in the Congress in 1950, there was some level of comity and understanding between the president and the Congress. But too often that is not the case now, whether or not the same party controls both branches of the government. And I think you can trace it essentially to one cause: the president has all but been cut out of the budgetary process.

The budget reform act of 1974 seemed like a good idea at the time. The elimination of impoundment and rescission authority in the president probably was inevitable under the circumstances. But the net effect was to take away the president's control of the national agenda in tax and economic and fiscal policy. Too often, the president's budget was simply declared dead on arrival. The Congress went on its merry way in passing its own budget, or in one case passing no budget at all. But to get rid of divided government and bring some degree of balance between the White House and the Congress, the president, whether he is a Democrat or Republican, has to be given more effective authority over fiscal matters.

That could be done in several ways. He could be given

rescission or deferral authority, a line item veto. A supermajority could be required to override a president's recommendations. The Congress might be required to first take up and dispose of the president's budget, and maybe to vote on the entire budget before voting on the parts.

There are dozens, probably hundreds of ways that I have never thought of to try to restore some level of efficiency into the presidential role in the budgetmaking process. But until you do, the riverboat gamble—a term I once applied, in a seizure of excess candor, to President Reagan's 1981 economic and tax program—is being played with a stacked deck.

I wish President Clinton well, but I would say frankly that he has very little control over what happens when his budget and his recommendations are delivered to the tender mercies of the budgetary, appropriating, and authorizing committees of the two houses of the Congress. That is what troubles me about divided government—not a division between Republicans and Democrats, but a division of authority on important issues like fiscal and tax policy—and foreign policy as well. The institutional difficulties in our system right now are so great that they virtually guarantee at least a partial defeat of even the best efforts of any president to bring coherence and relevance to a presidential budget. I think of my career capstone as being in the Senate, not in the White House, but notwithstanding that, I think the White House must have an enhanced authority to deal with budgetary issues in this country if we are to face them successfully.

How would you get the Congress to cede power back to the White House? I think the Congress understands—or can be made to understand—that the budgetary process right now is in dreadful shape and something has to happen. It will be difficult, but not impossible, to convince Congress that the president under the Constitution is the only unified authority for submitting a budget for the government of the United States and that his budget should be accorded a higher status than it currently has. That would require not a constitutional amendment but only an alteration in the budget act. It would be no more difficult to do that than to try to impose discipline on the Congress itself. Congress probably understands that with 535 people in the budget process now, there is very little hope that self-discipline can be imposed from within the organization.

A secondary benefit in delegating rescission and deferral authority would be its powerful effect on those legislators who would be afraid the president was going to impound or rescind funds for their pet projects, which are still what makes the world go around in the Congress. If the president had the authority to do that, it would have a marvelously concentrating effect on the legislative mind.

Some of my former colleagues, especially Senator Byrd, will be violently opposed to that, on the ground that it fundamentally changes the constitutional balance on fiscal affairs between the Congress and the White House. But my reply is that if we do not redress the imbalance that has gradually developed over the last several years, we are never going to get a rational budget.

If we begin with discretionary spending and that works pretty well, the authority could be extended later to tax expenditures. But the Constitution is specific on the sole authority of the Congress to lay and collect taxes. So, for the moment I would settle for doing something with discretionary expenditures, even if that is an incomplete solution.

Senator Baker gave only faint support to a constitutional amendment to require a balanced budget:

I think the balanced budget amendment has a limited usefulness. I support it. But the most you can expect from it is to make it less convenient for Congress to spend in excess of revenue. I think it is impractical. It would be unwise to absolutely prohibit an imbalance, and most of the proposals for an amendment do not try outright to do that.

But I am afraid of a constitutional convention to propose a balanced budget amendment. I do not know how the delegates would be chosen. I do not think you can limit a constitutional convention, and I do not know what would happen to the Bill of Rights, or the separation of powers, or the balance of powers between the branches. I am afraid in this day and age of tinkering with the exquisite balance between our departments, which we can build on for an even more successful experience in the centuries ahead.

> *Lloyd Cutler agreed with Senator Baker on the undesirability of risking a constitutional convention. But, he added, "I do not share even his limited enthusiasm for a balance-the-budget amendment. That is simply like asking a drunk to sign a temperance petition. Of course he would do it—between drinks."*

> *David Gergen saw some usefulness in the movement for calling a constitutional convention:*

I realize there are a lot of dangers in a constitutional convention, but I am more open-minded about it. Particularly if this Congress and this president cannot deal with some of these issues, the threat of a constitutional convention can be very useful. In the last few years, a number of citizen-led movements have sprung up to try to change things here in Washington, and by and large they have been healthy. One may disagree with the term limits movement on the merits, but it has been a good way to send a message to the elected representatives that people are demanding changes, that they want tougher action.

Similarly, the Perot movement has had its beneficial effects. The Concord Coalition has been very helpful. These movements, by forcing the system, have made it possible for Bill Clinton to go to the public today and ask for tax increases and hear people say they want it. That would not have been possible four or five years ago. Today, it is good politics to ask for tax increases.

> *Barbara Sinclair saw the Clinton presidency as a "last chance" to make the American system work, with an unlikelihood of "orderly constitutional change" in the event of failure:*

Clinton and the Democratic Congress have got to produce. They have got to tackle those problems of most concern to Americans in a responsible, timely, and fair fashion, and they have got to make some discernible progress. People have got to see that we are moving in the right direction.

A failure to do that would indicate a deeper problem that no amount of tinkering with internal congressional structure can fix. Democracies have difficulties making hard choices. After all, hard choices are, by definition, ones where every option is going to make some sizable segment of voters unhappy.

Our constitutional structure with its division of powers severely exacerbates the problem of making hard choices. Given the extent of Americans' disillusionment with their government, this may very well be our last chance to make our system work. And if it does not, the result is much more likely to be a Ross Perot, term limits, and other such nostrums than it is to be orderly constitutional change.

In concluding the conference, moderator Hedrick Smith summarized the contrasting views of the meeting's optimists and pessimists. The optimists, notably Thomas Mann and Howard Paster, anticipated that President Clinton would turn out to be politically skillful, that the Democrats controlling both the White House and the Congress would have a sense of shared stakes, that the party was much more ideologically homogeneous than it had been in recent decades, and that the public was now in the mood to support reform and change. The pessimists, on the other hand, pointed out the weakness of President Clinton's coattails compared with those of successful Democratic presidents in the past, and questioned whether the public mood was indeed in favor of governmental activism. Smith was struck with the fact that among the pessimists were two who were "in one way or another . . . affiliated with some of the most effective, best-known, dynamic leaders in American history": James MacGregor Burns, as biographer of Franklin Roosevelt, and Kenneth Duberstein, as congressional liaison officer during Ronald Reagan's early, most successful years.

Looking ahead to the planned second conference, Smith observed that the initial meeting had produced "a very thorough menu of reforms": constitutional changes, party reforms, campaign finance reforms, a uniform primary day for congressional nominations, and perhaps even a constitutional convention. At the second conference, those meeting will look back upon the record of unified party government under President Clinton's leadership and, as Smith said,

disagree and debate about what President Clinton and the Congress did or did not achieve, and why or why not, and then try to understand in a period of united government after divided government—at least in party terms—whether or not our system has worked, can work, and what should be done about it.

Index

71